To Cory & Kim

Enjoy the Read!

Beryl
&
Bernie

RusticoRiders Cycle Africa

From Cairo to Cape Town

Beryl Doiron with Bernie Doiron

authorHOUSE®

AuthorHouse™
1663 Liberty Drive
Bloomington, IN 47403
www.authorhouse.com
Phone: 1-800-839-8640

First published by AuthorHouse 11/18/2009

ISBN: 978-1-4490-4972-0 (e)
ISBN: 978-1-4490-4971-3 (sc)
ISBN: 978-1-4490-4970-6 (hc)

Printed in the United States of America
Bloomington, Indiana

This book is printed on acid-free paper.

THE BICYCLE IS THE MOST EFFICIENT MACHINE EVER CREATED:
CONVERTING CALORIES INTO GAS,
A BICYCLE GETS THE EQUIVALENT OF
THREE THOUSAND MILES PER GALLON. — BILL STRICKLAND

TO BRENT AND BRAD

TABLE OF CONTENTS

FOREWORD

IT WAS A RATHER CHILLY MORNING ON JANUARY 12, 2008, WHEN I LOOKED INTO my helmet mirror and saw the Pyramids of Giza fade into the distance. Bernie and I were in the company of 55 other like-minded people from thirteen countries, on an experience that in many ways would change our lives. Little did we know what was ahead of us, only that this tour had taken place annually for the five previous years, so not getting any younger; we decided that 2008 would be our year.

Our winter of 2008 was unlike any other. We cycled south from Cairo to Cape Town for four months – through the deserts of Egypt and Sudan, the mountains of Ethiopia, the grasslands and lush rolling hills of Tanzania, Malawi, and Zambia, the dry flatlands and game farms of Botswana and the beautiful desert canyons in Namibia, and on to our destination, the fertile lands of South Africa into Cape Town. Never once doubting that we would not complete this journey, our winter turned out to be a very enjoyable summer. We do have a story to tell.

ACKNOWLEDGEMENTS

The people we encountered throughout the continent along the dusty roads and in the villages, towns, and cities on our pathway have certainly struck a chord with us and we must thank them for sharing their lands with us for this short period of our lives. In appreciation of their friendliness, a portion of the proceeds of this book are being donated to WaterCan, a registered Canadian charity dedicated to providing clean drinking water to some of the world's poorest people.

The fellow cyclists from all parts of the world with whom we spent four months became our family. They will be fondly remembered and we hope to continue conversing with everyone. The tour operators who looked after us like parents certainly deserve a mention as well.

We also acknowledge and thank Rae Simpson, Ursula Haas, Rick Goodfellow, Alak Goswami, Spiros Analytis, and Maria Abagis for sharing their pictures with us, as did many fellow riders, too numerous to mention.

Thanks to a chance meeting in a grocery store, I reconnected with D'thea Webster, a former colleague who was excited to hear about our adventures in Africa and offered her professional editorial services. Thanks, D'thea, for your editing skills, making the book sound even more like our own voices.

I'll be ever grateful to my husband, Bernie, who was by my side while cycling through Africa and also while writing this book. You might think that it seems more like my adventure with him as my sidekick. I often jest about Bernie in my stories and hope you will appreciate my doing so. Had it not been for Bernie's dream of doing this expedition in the first place, I probably would not have had this unforgettable experience. What I appreciate the most about Bernie on this adventure is that he took the chance in venturing off into the unknown with me, always looking out for me in his rear-view helmet mirror. He is my buddy and my roadster.

INTRODUCTION

North Rustico and Beyond

OUR BICYCLE TRIP THROUGH THE CONTINENT OF AFRICA IS ONE THAT WE WILL remember for the rest of our days. Our dream was to go on a cycling expedition where we would cycle consecutive days – we loved *the next morning*. In checking out cycling tours, we found Tour d'Afrique, a tour operating out of Toronto, Ontario, Canada – possibly the most grueling tour at the time. Thanks to technology we were fortunate to be able to follow the blogs of riders from previous years and literally connect with them; inspiring us to take on the challenge. Why not take on the toughest first, and in the meantime, see a continent. Cycling the continent of Africa was no doubt a daunting task, and better to sign up while we were reasonably healthy. It was exciting to think that we would be travelling a whole continent, especially in the winter months, and getting in shape at the same time.

Bernie and I are just two ordinary people, not rich, not athletic, fairly healthy semi-retirees in our early 60s. For the past few years, we've been spending May through October on beautiful Prince Edward Island, where we plan to reside when we are fully retired. During the winter months, we have been returning to work in Ottawa, enjoy city life, renew friendships; and of course, get out on the slopes to enjoy some downhill skiing.

We hope to inspire people just like you, to think outside the box and just go for it – whether it is cycling, hiking, walking, kayaking, sailing – whatever – just do it. I guarantee you will never regret your decision. All you need is good health and a keen desire to take on the challenge. Your health will actually improve. Cycling four months through a continent like Africa kept us busy and 'fit'.

Bernie and I both hail from North Rustico, (hence our website, rusticoriders.ca, and the title of this book), a fishing village on the north shore of Prince Edward Island, close to Cavendish Beach, where the well-known author, Lucy Maud Montgomery, gained her inspiration to write her world-famous books on Anne of Green Gables. I grew up in a rural community, just a mile from the village, a farming community that once supported a number of small family farms of which my family was one. I have 13 siblings – ten brothers and three sisters; all of us, in our younger years, kept busy on the farm. Bernie's background was more linked to the fishing community, mainly lobster fishing, in which his family is still active. There were six boys and five girls in his household – another good Catholic family.

Bernie and I were married in 1969, moved to Winnipeg for ten years, on to Halifax for a couple of years, then to Ottawa, where we lived for 25 years. We have two sons. Over the course of those years, we frequented gyms (on and off) and maintained a walking and running regime, but were not fanatics about it. When our children were younger, we spent our winters downhill skiing in the Gatineau Hills. I only mention this to give you an indication of our past fitness activities before embarking on this adventure. You can see that we were not athletes, just regular folk.

We started cycling more seriously around 2003, when we had the opportunity to live in the Gatineau Hills in Quebec, Canada, where we would jump on our bikes from our doorstep and within minutes were climbing the hills. Seeing this as a chance we could not pass up, we purchased hybrid bikes, a cross between mountain and road bikes. I recall the first time on mine; I had to practice in a local parking lot before my first jaunt, about 6km. Bernie cycled behind me, noticing my jacket (not a cycling jacket), unzipped and blowing in the wind – I was not the coolest cyclist around, but I thought I had really done well, a whole 6km. It took me a couple of months to conquer the hills, and I gradually found myself covering about 35km each time I set out. I was amazed and proud of myself to have gained the strength in such a short time. Bernie, of course, was a more seasoned cyclist; in fact, it was his prodding that got me on the bike in the first place.

We found ourselves taking extended cycling trips in the Maritimes, where we spent our summers, and realized that we enjoyed back-to-back days of cycling. Bernie had been following the Tour d'Afrique website since their start in 2003. After following the blogs of riders for a couple of years, we decided that 2008 was our year, and we signed up. We both loved cycling *the next day*, but we knew that this was extreme because the next day stretched into four months on a bike. What better way to explore a continent though – travelling with a tour complete with a cook, bike mechanics, a doctor and nurse, and support vehicles to carry our gear.

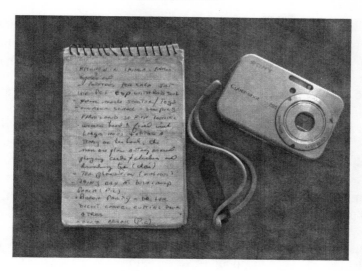

You will not find us embellishing our trip with a lot of fluff to make the tour seem more adventurous; rather, you'll get the facts firsthand. We made notes on the roadside and in our tent – in our little red notepad measuring 4x6 inches where only a single word was needed to jar our memory. This little notepad along with our camera were the only tools we had at our daily disposal, we became minimalists in every sense of the word.

We've included photos throughout the book that illustrate our stories but most often, the photos don't do justice to the beautiful landscapes we passed throughout the whole continent. The photos are in black and white, as it would have made this book far too costly had we insisted they be in color. You can go to our website (www.rusticoriders.ca) and find these pictures and many others in all their beautiful colors.

I must correct myself; I do embellish a little when telling some of my stories – you'll know when I'm pushing the envelope a little too much.

At the outset, I must mention that Bernie and I are authoring this book, even though I put myself as the first person in the text. The reason for this is simply that my fingers are on the keyboard, so I am writing it *with* Bernie. I do this for ease of writing and your ease of reading, rather than having Bernie writing on and off throughout the book, however, he does get to voice his stories now and then. I might add that I do not consider myself a writer; you might say, more of a *'teller'*, and we hope you enjoy our story.

Before embarking on this four-month tour, writing a book on our adventure was not in the plan. That would have made the tour itself too much like *work*. If we had started on the tour with such a goal in mind, we would not have enjoyed ourselves as much as we did, and we would not have taken the time to just *be in the now*, as I often say. Cycling across the continent into Cape Town was first and foremost on our minds. We did decide to keep in touch with family and friends through a blog, and I had taken on the role of scribe, putting together our blog entries, which was enough at the time. Before embarking on this tour, we decided to raise funds for WaterCan, a registered Canadian charity dedicated to providing clean drinking water, basic sanitation, and hygiene education to some of the world's poorest people. As mentioned, we intend to donate a portion of the proceeds from this book to WaterCan. As we are writing this book for publication in late 2009, economies are struggling all around the world. I'm certain, however, that the people we encountered, especially in the rural areas, are not consumed by the impact this economic downturn will have on their lives. One can easily notice that the divide between the haves and the have-nots, at least in Africa, is definitely widening.

We travelled with 55 cyclists who completed the whole tour (10,300km); this number increased when "sectional" riders joined us to complete certain portions of the ride. Our fellow riders hailed from all walks of life, from ages 22 to 68. Everyone appeared to be equal; all wore the same type of clothes (jerseys and cycle shorts), ate the same food, slept in tents, and rode bikes all day long. We found that no one really had a huge ego they had to fill – it truly was a pleasure getting to know our fellow cyclists. Everyone on the tour seemed to have a great deal of confidence in his or her own right. As a result, there was a lot of clever banter back and forth while on the road and around the campsite in the evening, as we all teased and cajoled each other. This whole experience allowed us to get to know the best and worst of each other and of ourselves.

Among the cyclists, 12 chose to enter a race of the whole continent, keeping a record of their daily times. We were numbered among the expedition riders – our intention was to cycle as much as possible, however, when sickness, injury, or just plain tiredness overtook us, we would take respite on one of the trucks, and we didn't have a problem doing so.

The tour operators consisted of a tour leader, cook, doctor, nurse, bike mechanics, drivers, and a media person, among others. The 2008 tour riders were also fortunate to be accompanied by a film crew of three, who cycled every inch with us and have released a documentary film entitled "Where Are You Go".

Living in the western world, we are constantly bombarded with news clips on happenings from areas around the world, places we always think we will never visit. And here we were, doing just that. We tried to keep an open mind on the culture of the people who were welcoming us into their countries. My first impression of most of the countries we visited is that, in many respects, the patriarchal system still has a firm grip on society, especially in the rural areas. As we cycled through villages and towns and met with these rural people eye-to-eye, we witnessed their struggles and the challenges of their daily lives, but still the majority had a smile, welcoming us along our path. It would have been easy for us to be judgmental, but we did not come to judge. Instead of finding fault, which generates negative thoughts and drains your energy, we cycled along with an open mind, just happy to be there.

The reason I mention our background is that, during the first month on our tour, I swear that I was reliving my younger years on the farm in Prince Edward Island, as the areas we cycled through brought back memories of those years. Being able to share them with Bernie was a hoot – he knew exactly what I was talking about, coming from the same area. His sense of humour was refreshing. We did not put any pressure on ourselves and were joyful during the whole trip; we did not try to excel over others, did not set goals, we just enjoyed *being,* every day. We belonged to the present, all ambition left us.

Readying for take-off

We are two very healthy individuals after receiving all our immunizations: Tetanus, Diphtheria, Polio, Typhoid, Hepatitis A and B, Yellow Fever, Meningitis, and Rabies, along with the malaria tablets we were to take weekly. We had to secure visas to enter Sudan and Ethiopia before leaving Canada. For all the other countries, we would purchase a visa at their respective borders.

We had the opportunity to visit with a former Tour d'Afrique rider who rode the continent in 2007. We gained many tips; from types of tires to Chamois Butt'r (a cream designed to look after our butts). And, oh yes, never ever forget toilet paper and baby wipes as the first two months on the tour we would be sleeping in many desert camps and, as we moved further south through the continent, many bush camps. Of course, we would be able to replenish supplies like this; however, we learned that the first month or two, supplies might be hard to come by. We learned about the Schwalbe tire, manufactured in Germany, among the best for cycling in Africa because it is puncture resistant. As Africa is a thorn-infested continent, we invested in two sets of tires and a spare each for rotation purposes, which proved to be one of our best purchasing decisions. So, all packed and ready to go: camping equipment, Giant Rainer mountain bikes, spare parts, casual and bike clothing, toiletries and first-aid supplies, computer, batteries, iPods, cameras, with toilet paper stuffed in wherever we found an open crevice. Our friends and relatives couldn't believe how light we were travelling, and to think we would live with these meager supplies for four months.

After enduring four snowstorms in the last week before our departure from Charlottetown, P.E.I. on January 7, 2008, we got off the runway without a delay. During an eleven-hour stopover in Halifax, we spent time with friends before departing for London, Frankfurt, and our destination, Cairo – a total of 36 hours of airport and airtime. During our seven-hour stopover in Frankfurt, we took advantage of purchasing some time in the fitness centre at a nearby hotel. Bernie worked out while I just flopped on one of those lounges by the pool and fell asleep. Because of my nap, I had a great flight from Frankfurt to Cairo gazing at the stars most of the time. The ground seemed to be lit up from start to finish with small villages, towns, and huge cities. I'm an avid sky watcher – love the stars and it seemed that I wasn't far from home, because the sky I was familiar with on PEI looked identical to the one I was gazing at while flying over Europe. It dawned on me that we live in a very small world – it's just how you look at it. Bernie managed to find four empty seats in a row – so you know what he was doing.

The arrival at Cairo airport deserves a mention. After gathering our luggage and bikes, which arrived without incident, we breezed through customs and met up with a fellow cyclist who would be joining us on our tour and who, of course, would be using the same passenger van to our hotel. We headed off to the parking lot with the help of three guys who loaded our luggage on top of the van, asking us if we had any bungee cords to secure the luggage, obviously, they didn't – imagine! We did have some, but we were not about to open our luggage in a dark parking lot to retrieve them. The next problem: where were we going to put the bulky boxes containing our bikes? I suggested that they put them in the van and we would squeeze in alongside them, as I did not think seat belts were likely mandatory in Cairo. They managed to get two boxes in and then stood around wondering where to place the third one. My next suggestion was that they move the driver and passenger seats forward and put the last bike box behind the seats. I'm telling you this because you don't see too many women working around the airport – it's all men, and they don't usually take advice from women – so naturally, we had a laugh. Especially as they took my advice and it worked!

Up until now, I hadn't realized that this would be the last time any make-up would appear on my face for four months. Even my ever-present earrings and gold neck chain were tucked away until we reached Cape Town. Bernie and I were taking a big chance as well – living in a tent for such a long period, something we had not done for 40 years. I often said that we would either return with a renewed love for each other or ready to file for divorce. Well, we're collaborating on writing this book, so you know the outcome. We arrived in Cairo on January 9, which gave us some time for sightseeing and meeting fellow riders who were arriving from all parts of the world. After a few days of acclimatization, we would hop on our bikes on January 12 and head out on our four-month trek to Cape Town – we must have been nuts. Obviously, we'd do anything for a tan.

We cannot possibly share all our experiences during these four months, and I'm sure our fellow cyclists probably wouldn't want us to. We also don't want you to think that we're authorities on how to cycle on any tour. We're not trying to say we are right; nor are we trying to win or profit from this book, or trying to persuade you to walk in our footsteps.

Throughout the text, where I have taken you back to actual time, you will notice the text is indented. Where Bernie speaks throughout the book, the text is indented and in italics.

All mention of currency is in US dollars.

EGYPT — LEAVING THE PYRAMIDS

Getting in Shape on the Flat Roads!

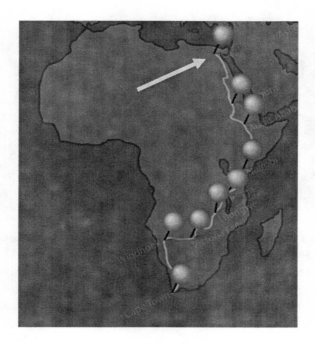

Entry: January 12, 2008 Exit: January 22, 2008	
Rough Roads (clay/washboard/sandy) – km	0
Pavement – km	1,002
Total Distance – km	1,002
Number of Cycling Days	8
Population – millions	80

BEFORE DEPARTING ON OUR AMAZING JOURNEY, WE VISITED DOWNTOWN CAIRO. What a city, with loads of history. The 'city that never sleeps' demands a visit all on its own; therefore, I will not go into much detail describing Cairo, except to say that it has great coffee.

After a 10km convoy from our hotel through the streets of Cairo and up to the Great Pyramids of Giza, we were greeted by press and various dignitaries, followed by a short photo session before we embarked on our journey. We had a military escort for all eight cycling days in Egypt, a precaution that Egypt takes to protect its tourism industry. We couldn't wait to get on the road and out of the city. The first half of our route in Egypt was along the Gulf of Suez and the Red Sea, and we were looking forward to the flat terrain. The paved roads would also be less taxing on our bodies at the outset of our tour, especially as we hadn't had much conditioning, leaving Canada in the dead of winter. On previous tours, the riders were welcomed on day one with a favorable backwind.

We found ourselves slowly gliding down the hills from the pyramids, jostling for room among the camels and their operators. Our first day was one we will all remember; unlike previous tours, we were handed a horrible headwind right from the start, while passing through the outskirts of Cairo into the countryside. A number of us had to be picked up by one of our tour trucks, as it was getting dark and the tour operators were very strict that no one would be left 'in the dark' to negotiate their way to camp.

Before I go on, I must mention that many riders were hoping to cycle the entire tour without ever having to hitch a ride on the truck, to maintain their EFI status (Every Fabulous Inch) – we often substituted another word. Bernie and I were not upset at all after losing that status on day one, because we hadn't planned on accomplishing that feat; however, a number of cyclists were disappointed in their performance on their very first day and knocked themselves around a bit. We thought we did pretty well – of the 128 total kilometers, we clocked in at 115.

Part of our orientation on the tour included instructions on what we had to do while cycling to let the tour operators know when we wanted to hitch a ride on the truck, because of injury, sickness, or just plain tiredness. When one of our trucks approached to pass a cyclist, the driver

would beep his horn and the cyclist would give a thumbs-up if all was OK, and of course, a thumbs-down if he or she needed assistance or wanted to catch a ride to camp. I won't speak for Bernie, but I'll tell you that I didn't have a problem giving the thumbs-down signal throughout the whole of Africa, although we hadn't expected to do so on the first day.

We entered camp after sunset and then had to find a place to set up our tent with only the light from our headlamps. Welcome to Africa; what have we gotten ourselves into? Things picked up after that first day, with a tail wind on days two and three – which meant that we reached camp early. In fact, on day three, we had time to take a walk along the shores of the Red Sea and dip our feet in – very cold – like the Gulf of St. Lawrence in June.

Speaking of the Red Sea, we saw beautiful resorts in various stages of building along its shoreline – I guess in preparation for the onslaught of retiring baby boomers from around the world.

Camping proved to be a bigger challenge than the cycling, at least at the outset. I swear I packed and unpacked our clothes a dozen times before leaving on our tour – I thought I had all the answers when it came to managing our stuff. Well, I was wrong. The first night at camp, everything was thrown around, looking for this and that – we had far too many clothes. Oh well, the first week is a test – things would run smoother as time went on – we hoped.

Tour d'Afrique prides itself on being a tour that does not leave its footprint in its wake. Apart from the tour vehicles, no one used fossil fuel energy to cross the continent. We also took great care in not leaving our garbage and waste for others to clean up; the tour led by example. Leading by example meant that each one of us carried a trowel, or used the tour 'shovel', for bathroom purposes. When nature called, we had to dig a hole, sometimes in the rock-solid desert floor, and cover up our "job". Tour d'Afrique's policy was that we were not to leave any sign that we had spent the night in any of the desert and bush camps we were about to use across the continent. Our conversations and laughter often centered on our toilet duties while we sat around on our three-legged campstools in the evening. All walks of life, all ages, but we all need a trowel.

Our route through the first portion of Egypt found us in total desert. It truly was an experience cycling along the flat roads where all you could see was sand, sand, and more sand. We rarely saw any animals, birds, or insects and very few people in the countryside. We were constantly passed by tour buses and a number of big trucks blowing their musical horns, which I believe they love – we hear them through the whole night and wonder who they are honking at. I was 'drafting' so close to Bernie in the above picture, you can't see me, only a small bit of my shadow – must have been one of those 'headwind' days.

To those readers who may not be familiar with the term 'drafting', I'd like to explain the technique commonly used in a peloton of bicycle racing. Usually when cycling into headwinds, I would ride much closer to Bernie, who wanted me to be within a few inches of his wheel, but I was too timid for that, opting for a foot or more of space and sacrificing some lost energy rather than a nasty fall for both of us, no doubt. A cyclist riding in the slipstream of another cyclist will expend 30 to 40% less energy than the rider in front. My drafting technique was basically having Bernie block the headwind. As an aside, there were times went he truly broke wind, especially when his stomach parasites worked on his fruit diet.

The courteous way to draft is for each cyclist to take his or her turn in the lead position. I drafted Bernie for the entire four months, never taking the lead position. We agreed that on our next adventure, our positions would be reversed.

At night the camp site becomes a city of tents – there are 63 riders (full tour and sectionals) along with 12 staff members – and almost everyone has his/her own tent – save for about seven couples who share. Our campsites in Egypt are mainly desert camps with no facilities; therefore, we have not showered since leaving Cairo and will not see showers or toilets for four days, until we reach the town of Safaga on January 15. It gets very cool in the evening (about 5° Celsius) and does not warm up until we're about an hour on the road the next morning, so we have to bundle up while at camp – no fashion shows on this trip.

I would be remiss if I did not share this incident with you. One night, while sleeping under the stars in the Egyptian desert, Bernie had to leave the tent around 1:00 a.m. to have a whiz – it was cold and windy, sand blowing everywhere. He had to put on his sandals, jacket, and long pants. Unfortunately, while exiting from the tent, the silk liner in his sleeping bag somehow got attached to the velcro on his jacket and it went with him, unnoticed. Upon returning, he undressed and readied himself to get back into his sleeping bag, but no liner. Of course, by that time, I was awake. We searched everywhere, tore the tent apart, whispering to each other – where was it? We finally decided that it must have gone out with him. He had to get dressed again and go looking for it in the total darkness, using only his headlamp. We hoped it would still be out there, maybe caught on one of the small thorn bushes that adorned the desert. When he got back, liner in hand, he told me that a wild camel had been about to munch on it and, in the nick of time, he managed to tussle it away from the camel with one swift kick from his now powerful biker's leg.

After cycling 110km on day four through the Eastern Desert Mountains, we were pleasantly surprised to find a hotel room in the town of Safaga, where we had use of a shower. Bernie was particularly thankful for the hotel, as he hadn't been feeling great the past couple of days. He checked with the doctor and found out that he had picked up a bladder infection, so we decided to take some time off and hitch a ride on the truck. We had an unwritten rule to stick by each other through sickness or injury, so, on day five, I jumped on the truck with Bernie. We had a great time; remember we joined the tour as expedition riders, not racers, thus placing no pressure on us to ride EFI.

Travelling into Luxor, we found ourselves on a route close to the Nile River, bordered by farmland. It was great to be out of the desert for a while, especially with Sudan still ahead of us. The farms along the Nile were very poor – most houses were incomplete. We learned that if the roof was not totally erected, the government could not apply property taxes, so completion rarely took place. We saw more of these 'missing roof tops' on apartment complexes in Cairo.

Our rest day in Luxor started with a welcome breakfast, including omelets and hot coffee, a step up from our daily dose of porridge. We were among 30 cyclists who went on a bus tour to the Valley of the Kings and the Valley of Queens, where we visited three tombs. Our tour guide was very informative and we spent seven hours on the tour. This historic sight deserves a two-week tour, an experience all on its own. Our tour lasted a little longer than we thought, leaving less time back at camp for bike maintenance and laundry duty, what would become a never-ending chore (not complaining, that was pretty well all we had to do).

While having dinner one evening at a local restaurant in Luxor, we met a very personable young man, about 20 years of age, who was getting married the next week – an arranged marriage. It was interesting to get his take on it – it seemed so natural to him. We again realized that, to appreciate their lives, we had to keep an open mind.

Bernie's bladder infection cleared up and we were eager to jump back on our bikes. We left Luxor, cycled about 130km to Idfu, and camped in a soccer field. We walked around town – it was like a town you would find at the time of Christ – the market was something else, with donkeys and wooden carts as the main mode of transportation in the market area, and cats all over the place. We continued to enjoy the coffee, and I wasn't missing my glass of red wine. We negotiated (bartered) the price for whatever we bought; however, everything was very cheap. I found, when we bartered, that we were at least speaking to a person, making eye contact and usually having a good time. It seems that back home in Canada, when we decide to buy something, we just hand over the money, get our change, say thank-you, and walk off. No discussion, sometimes not even eye contact, therefore, not nearly as much fun.

During each day, we had lots of time to think while cycling hour after hour, and one day, I had a brainstorm. Some of those big corporations should think about sending their senior management team on a tour like this one, somewhat shorter perhaps, a good team-building project. One has to be a real team player while on the road. The teamwork needed to set up a tent is a challenge, but Bernie and I got so we each knew our jobs so well, we didn't even have to talk to one another anymore while setting up camp – just short sentences. "Bernie, come here". "Beryl, where's my headlamp?" Also, everyone is equal. There's nothing much more humbling that digging a hole and squatting in the desert; we soon realized that we were all equal in doing nature's business, albeit in different surroundings.

After leaving the pyramids, we cycled on flat highways along with many vehicles, mostly trucks and tour buses travelling from Cairo to Luxor and their drivers did not slow down for us cyclists. Bernie had one close encounter on the two-way highway. One of many tour buses was passing him just as he was meeting an oncoming bus. The highway was wide enough to allow a foot or so distance between him and the passing bus. The clay shoulder is very wide and generally available for a quick escape. However, just as the buses and Bernie met, a half-ton Toyota truck, shocked Bernie by passing him on his 'right' on the shoulder of the road doing about 130km per hour – this was just too close for comfort. Bernie was caught in the middle, luckily all vehicles, and Bernie, met and passed without incident. I always say that if you're afraid to cycle in traffic, you shouldn't be there, and rear-view helmet mirrors are highly recommended when cycling on any roads. We all cycled through Egypt without incident.

Leaving Idfu, we cycled down to Aswan with the steady traffic and the locals carrying loads of sugarcane on donkey carts. We camped in a rather nice campground with grass (dried up) and, more importantly, flush toilets and hot showers. Because of our large group, by the time we had our showers, the water was a tad cool, something we soon got used to. We went grocery shopping and with sixty people converging on one small grocery store, about twenty feet wide and forty feet deep, the owner was all smiles, as the average purchase was about $30. Grocery shopping was essential, as we were going to have to augment our meals on the upcoming 18-hour ferry trip over Lake Nasser from Aswan, Egypt to Wadi Halfa, where we would be crossing the border into Sudan.

Since leaving on our journey, we sleep peacefully every evening and are both healthy. Bernie is back to his old self after getting rid of his bladder infection. We're a bit dirty, a reason for our good health; our immune systems have truly been tested. We have to say that we're not on a vacation; this is a total adventure and we are lucky that we both want to be here – it's as if we're paying for bootcamp. We are glad to say that we really feel safe with our military escort riding along with us.

There are a number of signs you will *not* see when travelling along the Egyptian highways, such as:

- no littering;
- clean fill wanted;
- no walking on the grass;
- don't pick the flowers; and
- restroom ahead.

In case you missed it, I repeat, you will *not* see these signs.

The 18-hour crossing turned into almost 25 hours, mostly because we had to wait for about 20 trucks to unload their goods onto the barges that were being towed by our ferry. Watching these trucks being unloaded was unreal – it seemed like organized chaos – no labour relations officer or union reps around; just bareheaded loaders, some even barefoot. A lot of shouting with no one apparently listening; however, the job was finally completed providing hours of entertainment as we watched from the ferry's upper deck.

The lower deck was wall-to-wall local people together with their luggage, all trying to find a place to sleep in this somewhat chaotic atmosphere. Our tour operators had purchased fares in advance, and Bernie and I were able to exercise our "senior" status and were allotted one of the twenty cabins. Comparatively, a cabin on the Joey Smallwood ferry that travels from Cape Breton to Newfoundland, Canada, is like the Queen Mary compared to our cabin, which was considered first class. About twenty of the younger people on the tour had to cuddle up on the upper deck, where every square inch was taken and, excuse me, every fart seemed just inches away.

While on the ferry, we were provided with a meal in the "dining room", which was non-smoking, except for the smokers. Each of us was assigned a one-hour guard watch where we had to monitor passengers entering our cabin area. I had a good time on my 'guard duty' stopping men from coming into our cabin quarters, men who ordinarily pay little attention to women. When someone (usually male) who was not part of our tour attempted to enter the cabin quarters, I would hold out my hand and place it on their chest, holding him back. It was fun; you should have seen the look in their eyes, startled that a woman would be so bold to do this to a man. I felt very secure, as I had some newfound Egyptian friends to back me up when I was in doubt as to who should be able to get through.

SUDAN — THE DESERT BECKONS

A "Dry" Country!

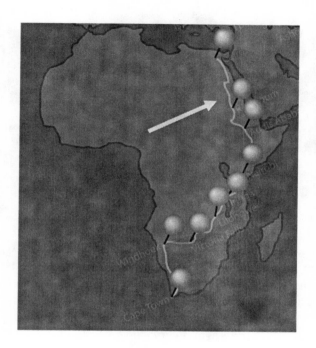

Entry: January 22, 2008 Exit: February 7, 2008	
Rough Roads (clay/washboard/sandy) – km	413
Pavement – km	1,107
Total Distance – km	1,520
Number of Cycling Days	12
Population – millions	40

UPON ARRIVAL IN SUDAN, WE WERE SURPRISED TO LEARN THAT WE WOULD BE spending an unscheduled day in the border town of Wadi Halfa, as the barge carrying our trucks would be arriving a day late. We took advantage of the delay to visit the town, and my thoughts went back to my younger years when the Bible played a very important part in my life. It seemed to us that the town had progressed very little since the time of Christ. Maybe we felt that way because of the desert all around, donkeys everywhere, mud huts with no heating, a charcoal burning pit for cooking, and no bathrooms – they were lucky to have a latrine. Being in the desert, the temperature fell around 6:00 p.m. and it was very cool until around 9:00 a.m. the next day. The mud, or in some cases concrete, used to build their homes (huts), retain the heat of the day, giving what you would call a cozy atmosphere in the evening, at least until it was time for bed.

While setting up camp, you see that we enjoyed many visitors watching us preparing our home for the night.

On this unexpected rest day in Wadi Halfa, we were fortunate to have a local historian along with many locals join us at our campsite. Of course, he was eager to talk about the history of the Nubian Desert where we would be cycling for the next few days. He went on to say if it was possible to irrigate the deserts in Sudan; this land would be perfect for organic gardening – I guess you would have to agree, as the land has never seen chemical fertilizer. Who knows, in the years to come, this obstacle maybe overcome and the lands will be irrigated, thus providing excellent land for food growth for the peoples of the world and great opportunities for the local people.

In most of the countries travelled, we saw women from the small towns and villages, and some even in the bigger cities, who had set up small businesses selling coffee, or other products. These women deserve a place in heaven – they are so kind and gentle, usually wearing a smile. They made great coffee, and every time we had a chance to partake of a cup, we didn't hesitate to leave a tip – they loved us. You have probably heard of Mohammad Yunus who started the Grameen Bank (both he and the bank were winners of the 2006 Nobel Peace Prize). The bank provides small loans or 'microcredit' for women to start small businesses, empowering them to change their lives. It also gives them hope instead of always thinking of 'just getting by' and instills a sense of pride in themselves.

Back in Luxor, Eqypt, we purchased each a *dress* – yes, Bernie too. In the Middle East, Bernie's dress is more commonly known as a *dishdasha*, so I gently reminded him that when he wears his dress, he had better be prepared to wash the dishes in a 'dash'. We thought it best to make the purchase, as they will come in handy in the heat of the Sudan, especially when arriving at camp in the mid-afternoon. It also serves as a good cover-up for me during our upcoming rest days in the cities and towns. While in Sudan, the female riders have been cautioned to cover their heads, and their elbows and knees are also not to be exposed.

Through the Eastern Sudan, our tents will be pitched on the desert floor – out in the wilds; no electricity or sanitation. Our water will be rationed, just enough for drinking and cooking for the next six nights, until we reach Dongola. Hey, no sweat, we haven't had many amenities since we left Cairo, we're getting used to it. Oh yes, there is absolutely no alcohol in Sudan – if Bernie wants to smuggle in some scotch, he risked the possibility of being shot.

Speaking of rationed water, most cyclists on the tour chose various charities or NGOs to raise money while on the tour for their particular cause. We chose WaterCan; an NGO headquartered in Ottawa, Canada, and have been raising funds since returning from our tour, including some proceeds from the sale of this book. This picture shows one of many roadside water facilities set up for the locals. The locals, of course, use it for drinking and cooking. We did not chance drinking it; no doubt, this water had not been treated.

Our iPods came in handy in Sudan; traffic was very light, especially for the first few days as we cycled on the back roads filled with soft sand. We departed Wadi Halfa on roads like the one in the above picture, confirming the fact that this was not a Sunday ride; one needed a mountain bike on these roads – we need to have our heads examined! If you look closely, you will see me in the picture riding solo.

There were quite a few falls – some fairly serious. When I get tired, I lose concentration, so I decided to minimize my falls and after 25km, I opted for the truck. This gave Bernie some freedom to strike out, as he often waited for me. After lunch, I decided to join him again and we went about 25km, when we both signaled thumbs down and jumped on the truck. This stuff is for the 30-year-olds – they actually had fun.

The desert is quite spectacular – like the surface of the moon. This picture has to be one of my favourites; having just set up our tents, we are now waiting for dinner. It's difficult to describe the feeling of living like this, the simplicity of living *'in the now'* with no outside interference – we don't even know what day it is.

I think we have mastered this 'tenting' thing after being on the road for almost two weeks. Since leaving Cairo, it seems that camping was more of a challenge than cycling. We're finally organized and everything goes in the same place each evening. It is quite a routine – we set up and break down in the same fashion each evening and morning; we have never gotten along better; life is so simple. However, when Bernie is using his wipes in the tent, I still have to remind him "face first"! One evening, while dozing off to sleep in the quiet of the campsite, Bernie asks me; "Beryl, if a woman speaks in the middle of the desert, and no one else is around to hear her, is she still right?"

While touching on the subject of hygiene, I knew I would need a couple of days with an esthetician when I got back to Canada – and that was only after two weeks – imagine after four months! Before leaving on this tour, I jokingly mentioned to my friends that one of the reasons I was doing the tour was that I would not have my hands in dishwater for four months, so my nails would be just perfect when I arrive back home. I was wrong; just being on the road for two weeks, my nails were cracked, covered with hangnails, and dirty. Bernie said he had never had so many toiletries in his life as he did on tour – he feels like an Avon salesperson.

This was one of the many coke/coffee stops we gladly sat down at all across the continent. We always looked forward to this much-deserved break, meeting fellow riders who had either found the café ahead of us or joined us while we were enjoying our break. It was a pleasant thought to think that we would be cycling for four months, stopping wherever we could find a coke/coffee stop and meeting up with fellow cyclists, a great time to really get to know each other. It also gave us a sense of security, meeting each other on rest days in the streets and cafés of the towns and cities all along our route.

We have been on the road for a couple of weeks now and I'm getting worried about my life with Bernie on this adventure – I think he's trying to get rid of me. As I said, Sudan is a dry country – no alcohol – and you recall I mentioned that Bernie should not think of smuggling in any scotch. Well I have to tell you this. On our last rest day in Egypt, when we were able to get our permanent bags off the top of the trucks, I noticed something not so nice in my bag. Our permanent bag is only to be opened on rest days, as it does not have articles we need while riding in between rest days. When I opened my bag, lo and behold, a bottle of scotch was staring me in the face; and I don't drink scotch. I caught him in the act trying to use my bag to smuggle his booze into Sudan. Had the Sudanese border officials searched my bags and found Bernie's scotch, I believe they shoot anyone trying to enter the country with booze.

We spent FOUR days negotiating just over 400km of washboard, rocks, and sand, in some places five to six inches deep, having to walk 200-300 meters, and even a kilometer on occasion.

After cycling these long four days on the rough roads where we took an absolute pounding, I list our casualties: Beryl, three falls – all on sand, no bruises. Bernie, one fall on sand. No flats or punctures, no trots, no hemorrhoids; so things were definitely not too bad.

We passed by a number of graveyards throughout the continent. In the graveyard pictured above, you will notice that each grave has pebbles around the headstone; as it is custom, when visiting your loved ones, to lay a stone by the graveside. While cycling by the graveyard, it struck me that the loved ones buried under these headstones should feel at peace. The saying *keep it simple* certainly applies here. You can imagine that these village people didn't get too stressed over the state of their graveyard, possibly because cattle could be walking through it and knocking down the headstones. The simple solution to that – just stand the headstone up again. In one village, we met a funeral parade where the deceased was simply covered with a white cloth and carried on a wooden funeral stretcher to the graveyard to be laid in the ground to rest — no funeral parlor to be seen.

We camped in the Town of Dongola for two nights where we took a much-deserved one-day break from cycling and walked the town streets. We set up our tents on the grounds of the town zoo; if the tortoise dies, they will have to close the zoo, it was the only animal remaining. We were kept awake on and off by the large numbers of wild dogs barking all night long – dogs that weigh about 40 lbs – running loose in packs; I guess there is no leash law in Sudan. There were also a number of donkeys braying throughout the night. These dogs and donkeys weren't zoo animals – just roaming the town; and, of course, we always heard the call to early

morning prayers on the loud speakers. While walking through the town of Dongola, we saw donkeys pulling carts with metal wheels; those poor donkeys.

The beautiful gals in this picture were among the many we met on the streets of Dongola, dressed in traditional clothing with happy smiles, giving us a very warm welcome.

While in Dongola, we enjoyed an outdoor bath in our red boxes, (containers that housed all our camping equipment while being carried on the trucks). Bernie and I worked together on this task; while sitting in my red box, I washed the clothes with soap and passed them on to Bernie who was sitting in his red box waiting to give them a swift rinse –

and we are paying for this! We then had to find a couple of trees to put up our clothesline. By the end of the tour, everyone knew exactly who the owners were of clothes on any specific clothesline.

Arriving at an 'internet café' was much anticipated and appreciated; however, there were usually several cyclists waiting to use the sometimes two computers, which meant you couldn't hog the keyboard. As I had brought my computer on the tour, I was able to prepare a piece for our blog and transfer it to a memory stick, saving time when I did get to a café. The internet was *so* slow though – I believe the whole continent is on dial-up service. Checking your email rivaled carrier pigeons for speed. The café, opposite, is one the poorest we came across on our whole tour. We learned that each year since the tour began in 2003; they have seen increased improvement all across the continent in technology access – of course, in some countries more than others.

> We have been on the tour for almost four weeks and have yet to experience rain – we haven't even seen a cloud in the sky. We know that this will change south of the equator when we enter Tanzania in the midst of their rainy season. I can imagine that will be fun, breaking down a wet tent. The mornings and evenings are still cool with temperatures in the low teens – the high of the day is usually in the low 30s Celsius.

While in Sudan, the female cyclists had to dress modestly and in accordance to Sudanese customs. When small children saw our female cyclists with exposed legs and arms, they yelled and pointed at us – no doubt, to them, we seemed almost naked. One day, when riding through one of the rural villages, I decided I just could not abide by this custom – it was simply too hot – and I took advantage of having Bernie riding close to me. I was riding slowly through the village and an older man, standing by a hut, caught my eye. He slowly rolled up his sleeves on both arms and tapped each arm with his opposite hand, then crossed his arms, letting me know that females should not go around with uncovered arms in Sudan. I smiled and cycled on and kept close to Bernie.

Many children, especially in the rural areas in Sudan and most other countries we cycled through, could be seen wearing western-style clothing. I have often wondered, as have many others, whether donations that have been directed to Africa over the past decades ever reached the people in need. Used clothing is one item that does make its way to these people; as you see western clothing on children, teenagers, and adults alike. In some villages, the clothes are piled high in the market areas, available for an extremely modest price. Bernie did see a child wearing a t-shirt that came from Peggy's Cove in Nova Scotia – I don't suppose his parents picked it up while vacationing there.

We will be cycling a four-day stretch (550km) into Khartoum, but hey, all new pavement, as the Chinese are assisting the Sudanese Government with their road infrastructure. We have noticed that they are in the process of building a divided highway with the hope of developing a tourism industry in the Northern Sudan. Anything is possible!

As we cycled through these very primitive towns, hundreds of waving and smiling children greeted us. Memories came back of the stories I heard in my younger school days about these children not having any toys and, you guessed it, they were still playing with a tire – no toys to be seen.

There was one exception to these smiling, happy children. While Bernie was cycling through a town, like the one in the picture above, two boys (about ten years old) had stones in their hands and when he motioned for them not to throw their stones; they waited until he passed and one of the boys threw his stone and hit Bernie. He jumped off his bike and chased the young lad into a house, through the bedroom and into the courtyard, where several adults approached him. After he explained what had happened, they said "sorry, sorry".

While cycling along the Nile, we noticed a number of crops being irrigated from the river – see the numerous palm trees lining the river, all surrounded by desert. The Nile is still a vital waterway transporting people and goods; evidenced by the number of cruise ships we see moving along its shores. We also find the fishing industry still alive and flourishing. The river is even a source of drinking water.

Since leaving Cairo, we have decided that we prefer desert camps over camping just outside of small towns or even in the bigger cities, for a number of reasons; one of them being there is no 'call to prayer' at 4:30 a.m. and 8:00 p.m., disturbing our much needed sleep. Every city and most towns we've been through have a call to prayer on loud speakers. People stop, face east, and pray while kneeling on their prayer mats – young and old alike.

Another reason we prefer desert camps is that it is much better when nature calls to just walk off into the desert, dig a hole, and cover your job, rather than having to use a latrine, which is usually full. One must always make sure to bring along tissue on these lonely roads, and, you guessed it, Bernie found himself without any. He had to use the only paper in his cycle bag – some souvenir Egyptian bank notes. With the current exchange rates, he didn't lose too much.

As you can see in these pictures, we set up our tents fairly close to one another. This made for mingling while working on bicycles, sharing tools, and just plain sitting around relaxing and chatting in a more secure environment than the roadsides cafés, where we took breaks during the day. You'll notice in the picture above, at this particular campsite, we had overnight security watching over us from the hilltop.

We had three days of strong backwinds while cycling from Dongola to Khartoum, distances of 140, 140, and 160km. The tailwinds were appreciated, but with it came blowing sand. We had three days of what we called an exfoliation treatment on our legs, arms, and face. Even our tattoos looked faded. The evenings were no better – high winds blowing sand everywhere – even found its way into our sleeping bags. I'm not complaining though – with all that backwind, it seemed like an effortless sail through the desert. A few of the riders had trouble with their cameras – the sand getting into the shutter retracting mechanism, causing it to breakdown.

Here we are enjoying our lunch at one of our many lunch stops along the route. There was no complaining at this particular stop – we were a happy bunch as we were just 'pushed in' by the great '3-day backwind' along the flat paved roads of Sudan.

While riding through the blowing sand, we met a man leading two camels, and as we approached, the camels bolted. The herder tried to hold on to them, but in a few seconds they were about 100 meters away from him, and we watched him chasing them into the desert. We felt bad about his misfortune, as I suppose we spooked the camels coming up from behind them on our bikes. No doubt, he had to chase them down several kilometers into the desert. Bernie said that if he had used 'scissor' bits on the camels, he would have been able to hold onto them. As a kid, that's what Bernie used in North Rustico, P.E.I. to hold on to Connie Simon's red mare.

The above picture does not illustrate this particular story; however, it gives you an idea of the expanse of the desert.

Further on down the road, we came upon a herd of camels at a watering hole, attended by a herdsman. We noticed that they hobble the lead camels by tying their leg at the knee joint while they are being watered so they do not suddenly take off, no doubt causing a camel stampede. We have not seen a fence in Sudan – in fact, very few fences in Africa, especially in the northern countries.

The day we rode into Khartoum was a short cycling day – just 100km. We had a very well organized 35km police convoy guiding us through the city; with traffic kept at bay as we moved through in one great peloton. People lined the roads the entire distance while cheering us on – a very warm welcome. We had officially completed the first section of the tour – Pharaoh's Delight. The total distance travelled was 1,960km, of which Bernie completed 1,680 and I managed to complete 1,550. Bernie was sick after just four days on the tour with a bladder infection and, as I mentioned before the tour, we had made a pact with each other that we would stick by each other through illness or injury. If we did not want to ride because of just plain fatigue, we were on our own in the truck – and that is what happened to me. I was nervous of cycling in deep sand for the first couple of days and cut back on my daily distance, because I didn't want to get hurt foolishly. However, I eventually got the knack of it toward the end of those deep-sand days. You might say it was a bit of fun – sort of like

skiing in powdered snow – just lean back on your bike and let the front
wheel ride up on the sand.

A Typical Day in Our New Lives

It has been just under a month since we left the Pyramids and we have, by this time, established a fairly strict routine in our daily lives. The picture on the previous page gives you an indication of the amount of "stuff" that comprises our home – and will for the whole four months – we are easily becoming minimalists. Once we have all our gear arranged in the boxes, we load them on the trucks, as shown above, to be driven to our next camp.

Our daily routine went something like this for the remainder of the tour:

- Rise at 5:30 a.m. – in the dark, as the sun rises about 6:30 a.m. In the nearby villages, the call to morning prayers is heard over the loudspeakers at 4:30 a.m. – a pre-wake-up call.
- Get dressed – we layer the clothes on take-off in the morning and after an hour on the road, started removing jackets, full gloves, and so on.
- Toilet duty and brush teeth – using water from our bike water bottle.
- Roll up sleeping bags, sleeping pads and pillows.
- Break down tent.
- Repack red boxes and load them on the truck.

- Replenish water and energy bar supply to get us to the lunch truck — usually a little over halfway to our next camp.
- Eat breakfast (porridge, bread, peanut butter and nutella, sometimes boiled eggs).
- Wash our dishes and tuck them in with our camping supplies.
- Lube the bikes.
- Hop on our bikes and cycle about 80km to lunch truck.
- Have lunch (usually pita sandwiches consisting of tomatoes, cucumbers, tuna, apples, oranges, cheese).
- Replenish water supply and fast fuel (electrolytes) to get us to our next campsite.
- Cycle another 50 – 60km to campsite.
- Upon entering camp, enjoy a bowl of hot soup to hold us over until dinner.
- Set up our tent.
- Prepare clothes for the next day (I never did that in my life, until Africa).
- Relax, read, and visit with neighbors.
- Eat dinner (choice of rice, noodles and meat or a vegetarian dish, bread, coffee, tea); it was like being at a dinner party every evening.
- Toilet duty and brush teeth. We mastered having a 'water bottle shower', that is when we weren't on water rationing.
- Snuggle into sleeping bag with your favourite book and headlamp (in the dark, as the sun sets about 6:30 p.m.).
- Because of drinking so much water while cycling, it goes without saying that we always had to exit the tent sometime during the night — making our way in the dark with the help of our headlamp.

Yes, a typical day – it took us about two weeks to get into the groove – life was so simple. I mention boiled eggs, they were especially welcome to stock up on at breakfast time, one in each pocket kept my hands warm while preparing to leave camp in the morning and later on, provided a mid-morning snack on the road.

We had two rest days in Khartoum, and decided to sleep in our tents rather than get a hotel room, as we were staying about 10km from the city centre in an international campground. It was well equipped, with outdoor laundry facilities – this picture shows our tent, with our bikes taking a rest beside it. It was easier to stay in the campsite than to hire a taxi to transport our gear to a hotel (cheaper too).

On our first rest day in Khartoum, Bernie gives the bikes a '2,000km check-up', and I do the laundry with the locals – scrubbing in buckets – this is only if we are camping and do not get a hotel. When we 'hotel-it', laundry facilities are usually available, but are not guaranteed. This morning I did the bulk of our laundry at the outdoor 'laundromat' with the locals. In the afternoon, I did another portion of my laundry and noticed that a couple of the women who were there this morning, scrubbing by hand, were still there, sitting on rocks scrubbing – imagine. I can do this, because I choose to do it on this adventure, but these women have washed their clothes in this fashion all their lives. However, they seemed happy, chatting away – I wonder if there's much to gossip about. They hang their clothes on a nearby fence and sometimes just lay them on the grass to dry; it reminds me of PEI in the 50s when we ran out of clothesline. With 13 siblings, that was quite often.

We also saw women sweep the grounds around the campgrounds, which also reminded me of living on the farm on PEI. In the summer, we had to sweep the ground around the back doorstep, because sometimes the cattle came a bit close to our house. Can you believe that this is still being done in the capital city of Khartoum in a tourist facility? Oh yes, they are still using hand-made straw brooms.

Today in the campground, one of the female riders didn't have her hair covered, and a man wearing a white robe approached her saying, "You're in Sudan, and you must cover up". Bernie asked if that meant him too, because his hair was somewhat unruly, but the man replied, "No, not you, just the women". There is no fear of anyone having to tell me to cover my head – no one has seen my hair since starting the tour. I've been wearing either a baseball hat or my helmet since the tour started. It's just not fair – the guys can dress as they dress in the west – it is 'freakin' hot here – but we gals are loaded down with clothes.

I may complain about some of the Sudanese customs, however, I must say that the Sudanese are really a very friendly and helpful group of people. Those living in the villages through which we cycled rarely see a tourist, or any foreigner. I'm certain that very few foreigners apply for tourist visas to Sudan, so you can imagine how these people react when seeing a group of cyclists, with all their colorful cycling attire, come cruising through their villages. We saw their curiosity, were met with their hospitality, and more than anything else, we did see happiness in their eyes. We have never felt unsafe on this trip at all – hope it remains that way.

On our second rest day, we found ourselves in downtown Khartoum visiting the street-side coffee stands where the women set up those small businesses I spoke about earlier. We spent our time just sitting around watching the people and traffic.

Upon departing Cairo, our mornings and evenings had been cool, sometimes very cool. Well, the mercury climbed; when we left Khartoum, the daily temperatures reached the 40s Celsius. I found out what it was like to cycle in that heat on the second day after leaving Khartoum. With a distance of 145km and a lunch stop at 70km, I made the lunch stop with some energy to spare, so gave it a shot to cycle the next 75km to the campsite, which made for a trying afternoon. About 30km from camp, I had to stop and sit by a hut in a village in the shade for about 15 minutes to regain my strength, making sure I was well hydrated. Bernie, while shooting a short video of the children in the picture above, took the time to talk with these children asking each their names. They were all eyes, had fun talking with him, and got quite excited while seeing themselves in his video.

After I regained my strength, I was back on the road for another 30 minutes or so when I had to rest again, feeling faint, this time about 20km from campsite. We found a large culvert that provided shade and, oh yes, we sat there among piles of donkey dung. Bernie had been very patient with me, and he must have been concerned, because after this rest he said, "Are you ready, Sweetheart?" He has never called me Sweetheart in my life! I reached camp on my own with no help from the truck. When we arrived in camp, some of our fellow cyclists asked us how we got along in the heat. Bernie replied, "Pretty slow; as a matter of fact, a dung beetle passed us – we started drafting him, but after a few meters he headed for the hills of sand – curses". It was good teamwork that got us to camp without any mishaps, and of course, Bernie set the tent up without my help that evening.

The evening brought an end to a grueling day and we took a chance of going for a swim in the Nile, after all, we were camping on its shores. This picture shows Bernie holding down a 15-foot crocodile allowing me to go for a quick dip after my grueling day – what a man!

In the early evening, most of us cyclists could be found relaxing in and around our tents waiting to hear the loud summons from Duncan, our tour director: Riiiiderrrr Meeeeeting!!! We would rise and grab our carefully guarded campstools. With the addition of sectional riders, the tour grew in number and the now 'seasoned' full tour riders were all too aware of the scarcity of unbroken campstools.

During the rider meeting, the following day's route, and specific instructions were recorded on a grease board, reviewed, and any uncertainties clarified. Occasionally, and most enjoyably, one of the tour support group members would provide an information session on the country and/or specific areas visited. From time to time, we also had a refresher course on the local language. When visiting a foreign country, I find that to be able to speak and comprehend even a few words in the local language will often open so many doors.

When the meeting was over, dinner was usually ready and those of us who were very hungry (usually Bernie) soon realized that one could listen to the meeting instructions while sitting rather close to the front of the soon-to-be-formed dinner lineup. Also, one needed to be close to the front of the line-up if you wanted a second dinner helping. The rule for getting seconds was simple, wait until everyone had gone through the line and the cook announce that 'seconds' were now available. One did not get seconds unless your plate was cleaned-up, so to speak. Second helping were often minimal, at least the meat, so in order to ensure availability, one had to be near the front of the first line, eat up at a steady pace, and line up for seconds. During the time of my stomach sickness, I was eating my own food that I had purchased. On the days when Bernie was exceptionally hungry, he would get two dinners, knowing full well that I would eat very little and then he could finish it off thus avoiding the line-up for seconds.

Before leaving this section on Sudan, I have to include this little tidbit. We decided that the national flower of Sudan had to be the plastic bag, small bags mainly used to carry bread — they are everywhere. There is no infrastructure for garbage pickup in the rural areas – you wouldn't expect it either, when there is little sanitation facilities – certainly that would come first. These plastic bags, thrown around the rural villages, get caught up in the small thorn bushes and just blow, blow, blow.

To sum up our trek through the deserts of Egypt and Sudan – this past month has taken me back to my younger years. There are so many likenesses to how we lived on the farm in PEI. Seeing the people in the irrigated fields from morning to evening tilling the earth and harvesting the crops brought back memories of the days on the farm. Back in the 50s and 60s on PEI, farm mechanism was present, whereas today in Northern Africa, farm mechanism is still almost non-existent. The sights I have seen on these first days of our journey have also brought me back to my younger years in school and church – our day was mainly filled with church and school-like activities, walking to and from school carrying our books without the aid of a backpack or satchel. And oh, I mustn't forget, every evening our whole family would all kneel in our living room and prepare to recite the rosary – not unlike the 'call to prayer'.

It has become commonplace to see women totally covered, rarely walking alone, and of course, never riding a bicycle. It makes me think that we are all connected, like brothers and sisters all over the world. During the late 50s when I was 10 or 11 years old living in a northern country, the winters were sometimes cruel. We walked two kilometers or so to school and sometimes had to wear long trousers for warmth. We were allowed to wear trousers, as long we wore a skirt over them; and girls were never allowed to enter church without a hat or scarf on their heads. Of course, there were times when we did not have either; so with a bobby pin, we would attach a piece of paper or tissue to our heads – memories of my past – traditions that are still evident today in some African countries.

The Bible stories I heard as a child had mostly taken place in the Middle East, so I sometimes feel like I am living back in those biblical days. The big question in my mind is: how come these people have not advanced? Then, who am I to say that they have not? We did see hardship on the faces of the people, but we also saw hope and happiness. While cycling, my mind has been quieted from the usual 'present-day' thought overload – long distance cycling will do that to you.

ETHIOPIA — INTO THE HILLS

Dodging Stones!

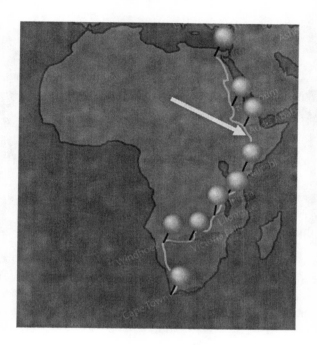

Entry: February 7, 2008 Exit: February 29, 2008	
Rough Roads (clay/washboard/sandy – (km)	578
Pavement – (km)	1,238
Total Distance – (km)	1,816
Number of Cycling Days	17
Population – millions	75

WE CROSSED INTO ETHIOPIA AT A SMALL TOWN CALLED METEMA. AS THIS particular border crossing wasn't one of the main entries into Ethiopia, the immigration office was comparatively small – an earthen floor with chickens running "free range". I will not try to describe their office equipment; let's just say it was meager. The tour operators had provided the office with a list of the names of everyone on the tour, and the clerks had to sift through pages and pages of names to find each person; no alpha order there. Some of the riders had to wait two hours for the processing to be complete – and it was hot. Hey, some good news – just around the corner from the immigration office, the locals were selling beer, cold beer, for about 50 cents a bottle. After going without a beer for two weeks, Bernie had five over the two-hour period. Fortunately, for Bernie, I have never acquired a taste for the stuff, so that meant more for him.

Having just left the deserts of Sudan where you couldn't purchase a drop of alcohol and where women were frowned upon for showing their arms and legs, we enter Ethiopia and were met with an offer of beer just inside the border. Not only that, but our campsite was within walking distance of a brothel. What a contrast! The campsite was like being on Old MacDonald's farm – cows, chickens, roosters, goats, dogs (plus, of course, feces from them all, including humans). A great welcome!

The brothel was also a welcome sight, not because of its obvious services, but for the simple reason that, for a small fee, showers were available. The showers were situated next to one of the brothel rooms, pictured on next page.

Many Ethiopian villages and towns that lie on the truckers' pathway have a brothel where the men make their nightly stops in that vicinity. I guess there is some truth in the belief that AIDS is spread along the truck route – we saw it with our own eyes – a part of their culture.

Our stay in the campground on 'Old MacDonald's Farm' was most interesting. When we were pitching our tent, we had an audience of young boys and girls from the town, ranging in age from four to ten years or so. Obviously, the older kids, roughly 14 years of age, did not want these younger kids around, possibly competition for them as they were looking for money from the foreigners. The older kids started throwing stones at the smaller children, an age-old way of showing who has the power. This was my first impression of the country as we fell victim to the stone-throwing children while cycling the hills and lush lands of one of the oldest countries in the world and Africa's second most populous nation. The call to prayer over loud speakers, donkeys braying through the night, dogs barking and roosters crowing to arouse us early in the morning are all memories of our first night in Ethiopia. No room for boredom on this trip.

The tour operators informed us that travelling in Ethiopia would not be everyone's cup of chai as there isn't much tourist infrastructure and that we wouldn't want to have need of medical attention, other than from our own doctor and nurse who were travelling with us. They assured us that the landscape is splendid, the people are welcoming, the sense of history is tangible, and you won't have to worry about crowds of tourists.

Another big contrast upon entering Ethiopia is the layout of the countryside – a drastic change from the desert to hills, hills, hills, and heat. The first day of cycling, at the 30km mark on rock filled, sandy and dusty hilly roads, I found myself doing a 360° pirouette on my bicycle while trying to keep from falling, but finally succumbed, landing softly on my rump on top of my bike, no injuries to me or my bike. A few kilometers down the road, Bernie and I stopped to enjoy an energy snack bar, and while standing on a loosely graveled slope, my foot slipped and I fell flat on my back and this time my bike had nothing to do with the fall. Just at that moment, we saw the tour truck coming over the hill and Bernie said, "For God sakes, Beryl, jump on!" I guess my body was telling me something, so I listened and got back to camp early. Bernie continued and although it was only a 100km day, it was his toughest thus far, on hard-packed dirt roads. As there was very little wind, whenever a truck passed, the dust usually stayed on the road for about 10 minutes or so; his bandanna came in handy as a filter. Many of the 'expedition' cyclists walked up the latter part of some of the steeper hills, and Bernie even hired some kids to push him up for a coin or two and surprisingly, some kids refused the coins, implying it wasn't necessary to pay them; they were just in it for the fun.

Our second campsite in Ethiopia was absolutely stunning – overlooking a gorge next to a small village. The people lived in mud huts and had to walk long distances for their daily supply of water. They spent their days working small plots of land where they grew vegetables and fruits for their daily sustenance – just getting by. We noticed that, compared to Sudan, the Ethiopian countryside was not littered with plastic bags and very little garbage to be seen; maybe because they live totally off the land. Where would they get the usual cartons and cans to leave lying around? When we entered the small village, we spotted a coke stop and soon their entire supply of (warm) drinks was snatched up by the cyclists. We learned that the price immediately went up when they saw us coming; something we really didn't mind, as it was still cheap. The higher we climbed into the hills, the more expensive the coke and fanta became – but hey, not complaining.

I believe the soft drink industry has a very good marketing plan throughout Africa. We learned that the towns are supplied with cartons of soft drinks, in bottles only. For example, a local vendor would be allotted 20 cases of drinks. On the next drop off, if the company did not get 20 cases of empty bottles back, say only 19, the vendor would only be able to purchase 19 cases, and so on and so forth. Because of this rule, we were never allowed to take our bottle of coke with us; we had to drink it at the coke stop. This was not a problem, as we welcomed the sit-down; even if it was on the ground, we were at least off the bike. Even in the poorest towns we passed through, they have a recycling program and I bet they don't even know it. These poor towns do not have the basic necessities of life, yet you can always buy a soft drink – what a marketing plan and it includes recycling. Furthermore, across Africa when we purchased a soft drink, the vendor always took great care in making sure we were present when he or she removed the bottle cap. I wonder whether this was another requirement of industry's marketing plan.

Getting back to that beautiful gorge where we set up camp on our second night in Ethiopia. We shared the space with cows and their dung, but we were getting used to that. That evening, the sky was utterly beautiful, so we decided to leave the rain cover off our tent, which allowed us to view the stars through the tent netting; it was stunning. Bernie noted that no one else had their rain cover removed, but it wasn't to maintain their privacy; it was so they wouldn't have to look at us.

For the next few days, we cycled through many small villages off the beaten track. Most of these villages had no power, no vehicles, and crowds of people walking everywhere. Scores of small children kept running after us asking for money, with a few of them throwing stones to get us to stop. When I say a few of them, it seemed like many, the population of Ethiopia is 75M and 42% of those are children under 12 years old. They are not at all shy to ask for money, and some adults do as well. When they realized that we were not going to give them money, they then started asking for pens. Bernie always told them that he had no money or pens; and if he did, he would be driving through Africa, not cycling.

Ethiopia is one of the oldest countries in the world, and Africa's second most populated. However, much of the country sees little progress, particularly the rural areas. While cycling from town to town, one cannot stop thinking that the rural people seem to have been forgotten; there is no sign of the government helping them. In Canada, I have seen many people migrating back to the country in their retirement years to enjoy what country living offers – not so in these northern countries of Africa. I would think that those living in the city, only managing to eke out a living, would be reluctant to return to the country to what appears to be dead-end subsistence farming. We were always reluctant to give the children coins, as that increases their dependency on begging on the streets as well as putting more pressure on cyclists following us. A number of cyclists would *high-five* the children, but I was hesitant. I did not trust the kids, as they would sometimes grab your hand and hold on to it and where did that leave you – flat on the ground.

Around the campsite one evening, one of the riders jokingly said that Ethiopia seemed like the 'land of the living dead'. You might think this sounds rather harsh, but it was really very funny. When nature calls while you are cycling along the lonely roads in the countryside with no one in sight, you might think it would be a good time to dismount and walk off into the thorny desert-like terrain to do your business. While squatted, more often than not, suddenly, children would be running toward you as if they were rising 'out of the ground', shouting "you, you, you"; "where are you go?" and "give me my money". We heard these short sentences quite often as we peddled through the country.

Today, we are on a rest day in Gondar – a fairly large town – staying in a hotel, although our sleeping pads are more comfortable than the beds. But hey, can't knock the privacy, indoor toilet, and shower – worth it. Our routine on rest days still includes bike maintenance and laundry. Bernie is busy doing his bike maintenance and I hired a local to do the laundry and passed on along a well-deserved tip.

About mid-day, Bernie and I go to a restaurant on a terrace connected to a hotel. As soon as we enter, we are greeted by three young men (ages 18, 19, and 33). They are very friendly and immediately notice Bernie's tattoo and are very interested in it. Bernie wears a tattoo on his left calf – a picture of his very first bike. They invite us to join them. They all speak English so we take them up on their invitation. The 33-year-old is a driver for one of the tour buses and could not spend too much time with us, as he had to return to work. The boys, though, are very talkative.

These boys are from the country and living in Gondar attending high school, not brothers – just friends. They tell us that their older friend is helping them out while they attend school. They live together in a house in the city and work as waiters in the early morning for about two hours, eat their breakfast at the restaurant, and package food for their lunch – all from leftovers. They earn about $6 a month. On the weekends, they sometimes stay with the mother of the 33-year-old man and do chores for her, as she is aged and needs help – she lives alone in a one-room house. The chores include looking after her garbage and helping with her shopping in the market.

We talk about everything – they don't have girlfriends, nor do they drink beer, since they want to get an education and hope to go to university and prepare for their future. They are very thankful that their older friend helps them the way he does. Before meeting him, their only employment was as herders in the countryside earning about $2 a month with no future. We learned that the 33-year-old man is married and his wife lives in the US; she sends these young guys clothes, of which they are very proud. As this is the dry season in Ethiopia, water is in extremely short supply. Of course, the boys can't afford to pay for water, and every Sunday they walk or run about an hour to a river to wash themselves and their clothes. They also spend much of the day praying (Orthodox Christians), because they believe that their only hope for the future is in their prayers and education.

We talked for about a half hour or so, they then invited us to the home of their older friend's mother, saying that she would prepare coffee for us in the traditional Ethiopian way. Ethiopia is known all over the world for their coffee. We thought about it for a moment and took them up on it – her home was about ten minutes walking distance. Her house, situated in a very poor area, was clean, with two sofas, two chairs, a coffee table, a cabinet that held all her treasures, and a bed. She proceeded to roast the coffee beans burning incense while doing so – the whole procedure took about 45 minutes. She opened her cabinet and took out two fancy china cups and served us coffee along with sugared popcorn. The boys sat with us and were so respectful of this older woman; it was touching. A couple of younger children, possibly neighbours about two years old or so, dropped by; the young boys were very gentle with these children, it felt good to be in their company.

After finishing our coffee, we thanked the older woman and Bernie gave her some money for her hospitality, which she gladly accepted. The boys then walked back to the street with us – Bernie wanted to give them a little something as well but they would not take it. Just a nice story – sometimes you have to take a little chance to see the better side of things.

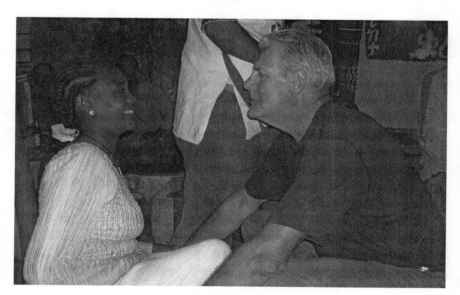

During our last evening in Gondar, a group of us went to dinner at a restaurant where two ducks walked around at their leisure throughout the restaurant. The food was typical Ethiopian – eating without utensils. Bernie said to the waiter, "Oops, I dropped my fork and serviette – just kidding". Then one of the cyclists from our group led us to a "shoulder dancing" club, and as you can see in the previous picture, Bernie found a lovely partner.

As the days pass and we leave the rough roads behind us, we look forward to cycling in Ethiopia's very scenic countryside. Our next four days are all on pavement, with plenty of hills and heat – we do expect to encounter more stone-throwing kids; it is a 'no-brainer' that I will stick close to Bernie. Mentioning stone-throwing kids, Bernie sure wishes he had his brother's potato gun – that would scatter them – he is working on a slingshot and will shoot grapes at them or more likely green olives – the hard ones. After being hit with stones, in frustration, we would often chase the kids, but can never catch them. If we ever did catch them, we thought we would march them home and have their parents/guardians discipline them, or better still take them to the police station to lodge a serious complaint. Sitting around the campsite in the evening, lately the conversation is about these kids. Bernie's suggestion, in jest of course, on how to transport them to the nearest police station without them escaping; is to duct tape the culprit to your back, so while still cycling, you could take him to the authorities.

I mention the hills, heat, and stone-throwing kids, as they are so vivid in my memory. In hindsight, those trials are what made our days unforgettable and why we cherished the experience so much – the memories are still so alive. Had it been a journey where everything was perfect, I don't know if I would be writing this book.

Ethiopia offered us a more diverse countryside than Egypt and Sudan, as there is a greater agricultural scene in the country. We noticed when entering Ethiopia that it seemed poorer than the first two countries we cycled through; however, the countryside in Ethiopia is far more beautiful; and this is their dry season. We see much less garbage as we peddle along, possibly, as I mentioned, because the people in the rural areas are mostly subsistence farmers and live totally off the land – so no cartons or other garbage to be left lying around.

When walking about our campsites, we almost never touched our bare feet on the ground, as we would invariably pick up a thorn – they are everywhere. These Ethiopians have been walking barefooted for most of their lives and the soles of their feet are like leather, no doubt. This reminds me of my early childhood on the farm where during much of the summer months we were often barefooted and boasted at being able to run through the freshly cut grain fields. The trick was to run at a very fast pace, thus lessening the prick of the sharp stubble. After running through a few fields, my younger siblings usually caught on to the technique (faster is better).

I must talk about the rural way of life in Ethiopia as we saw it. The people in the villages are very poor, having no means of transportation; they therefore walk from village to village carrying (usually on their heads) huge baskets of fruit, vegetables, or wood for making into charcoal. It was common to see women carrying baskets of cow paddies pilled four to five feet high, which they used for fuel. They headed to or from their fields where they toil all day or to the rural markets to sell and barter for food and other basic needs – no obesity problem in Ethiopia and Sudan. These young women always had beautiful smiles when meeting us. I believe the reason is that they would love to be doing what we were doing, riding a bike, as I haven't seen any women riding bikes since departing Cairo; not part of their culture. I often reflect on our experience and can see all those women throughout the whole of Africa, but especially in the northern countries, watching us pass by on our bikes – some smiling and waving – it is something I will never forget.

As you can imagine, the rural people live quite differently than we do in Canada. Living in a very warm climate, their houses, as we saw it, often consist of one room – to sleep in. Therefore, their 'home' really is the outdoors where the children are running freely and of course, they are fascinated with us – no such thing as cocooning in Africa. We passed through many small farms where these kids – yes kids – are working the fields; no sign of any mechanism, everything is done by hand. When the children saw us riding along, they would run from their spot in the field and race to the road to reach us before we cycled pass. They waved, shouted, laughed at us, and of course, asked for money. While running beside us, barefoot over very rocky soil, a few of them picked up some stones and threw them at us to ensure getting our attention.

It is hard to imagine that the country is still in this state, like going back centuries. The herders in the fields are paid roughly $2 a month to look after herds of goats, cows, and sheep – I imagine that includes their food and lodging. As mentioned, about 1% of the children will throw stones at us when we pass – just looking for our attention. I have switched to cycling in front of Bernie while in Ethiopia, so maybe the reason for us to be incident-free is because they see Bernie riding behind me and sometimes he stands up on his pedals. To them, he seems to be about seven feet tall, making them a little cautious about throwing stones; then, by the time they react, we're gone. Bernie decided to let his white beard grow hoping that the kids will spare him, seeing that he is an elderly person; so as a result, I get spared from the stones as well – I guess I'll stick with him. We have had a few stones thrown at us but they often have just rolled on the pavement as we passed by. We are very friendly with them, but do not stop to chat, as we would be swarmed – have to hold onto everything, as their hands move very fast. Many of these children have lost their mothers due to AIDS and some, if lucky, are being looked after by their grandmothers, while others are on their own.

A number of people on the tour fell to the stomach bug and jumped on the truck, Bernie was one of them. We only had 65km on the last day before reaching Bahir Dar where we were looking forward to having two rest days. We both left the campsite on our bikes in the early morning, but Bernie gradually felt weaker and weaker. He had been up a few times during the night and was not the only one feeling sick; about six people on the tour had been riding the truck for the past couple of days. Bernie went thumbs down, and jumped on the truck about 20km from our departure and I decided to cycle the rest of the day myself. I suddenly found out what a female, riding alone, may sometimes encounter. The kids saw me coming and because I was a lone female, they took advantage of the situation. They know they can overtake you on the hills; running alongside you for kilometers, continually asking your name and where you're going; and of course, letting you know that they needed money and pens. Most of them carry sticks and one youngster ran next to me for quite some time, pretending that he was going to poke his stick in my front wheel; he wasn't scared of me at all. Where was Bernie when I needed him? Further along, while cycling uphill, I approached a young boy about 12 years old. I smiled at him and a big smile lit up his face; however, when I rode by him, he urinated on me. I was shocked; he got me on my leg. I didn't get off my bike, just moved forward, and chalked it up to another experience.

Another incident occurred while I was riding down a long slope, a distance of about 3km. I came upon three pre-teens who were making a lot of commotion trying to indicate to me that there was something on the road that I would bump into if I did not stop – I slowed down, but then realized it was just a ploy to get me to stop; I rode by them without incident.

The Ethiopian people probably had as much reason to talk about me as I do to tell stories about them. One early morning, Bernie and I found ourselves working our way uphill through a town following a local cyclist and a pick-up truck with about five teenage boys sitting in the back open box. They were laughing and shouting at me, very friendly as they rarely see women on bikes. A local chap was riding ahead of me on his bike and I decided to overtake him – just to give these guys something to laugh at – they were cheering me on as I passed him. The poor guy will never live that down, a woman passing him on a bike. I then thought – what am I doing, so in order for the local chap to save face, I let him pass me before we got to the top of the hill.

While cycling through the many small towns and villages, riding behind some of the younger female cyclists from the tour, I would see young teenage boys bursting out laughing when the cyclists met up with them. Our interpreter, who sometimes followed along with us, told us that these young men were cracking dirty jokes about these girls as they rode by. I mention these stories to give you an idea of what the children were up to, but as I said, a very small percentage fell into this bracket; it just seemed like a great many because Ethiopia's junior population is so large. I don't suppose they see foreigners passing through their villages too often, and children, being children, are just looking for some fun – something for them to talk about while sitting around in the evening. We became their equivalent of computer games or television programs – they had to have some fun. The majority was very gentle and they were all nice-looking kids, dressed very poorly, most without shoes.

We were advised by our tour operators to avoid showing outward affection toward each other as we cycled through these first three countries (Egypt, Sudan, and Ethiopia). We noticed however, especially in Ethiopia, the men walk along the street holding hands with each other, and we learned that there is a good reason for this. A person will take another person's hand to get and hold his attention – the person listening is more inclined to listen to a person while his hand is being held – try it sometime.

We stayed at an older hotel in Bahir Dar; it must have been a nice hotel 75 years ago but needed a bit of maintenance. After checking into the hotel, Bernie suggested that I take my shower and he would look after getting our gear off the truck. I took him up on that, but he was up to his old tricks. The shower was very interesting; the water heater was situated in the shower stall with the plug coming directly from the wall. I suppose the wiring looked a little suspicious to Bernie and that was why he let me try it first. He seemed relieved when I made it through without incident. Oh yes, you also had to be very careful not to pinch yourself while on the cracked toilet seat. Oh well, our standards have dropped considerably.

While in Bahir Dar, the tour operators organized a "P" party, which took place in the bar in the hotel, everyone had to dress up in something starting with the letter P. There were popes, proctologists, a pyramid, a plant, a peanut-butter boy, a pygmy, a baby wearing a pamper, a picture, pimps and prostitutes. Bernie was a proctologist, with a sign on his back saying "The Assman". My costume was very simple; because I had been peed on the day before; I went as Ms. Peed-On. While at the party, I had a long chat with a local who was studying to become an accountant. This was the first time he had ever been at a costume party and he wondered why anyone would take the time to get dressed up in foolish costumes just for fun. Never seeing that before, he found it hard to comprehend. We partied and danced until midnight and the younger folks hung in until 3:00 a.m., as we were not cycling the next day.

When we left Bahir Dar, we started our five-day ascent to 3,000 meters. The first day we cycled to the lunch truck, about 80km, with the temperature reaching the low 30s. We had to walk a few hillcrests; our cycling was down to 5-6km per hour, so it was better to walk for a change. We cycled past some stone-throwing kids, as usual, but no direct hits. We stayed in a bush camp the first night, lots of cows and kids, so the tour operators roped off the camping area and they usually respected the ropes, the kids that is.

The following day, about 10km from our next campsite, we had to take relief on the truck, as the high elevation was just too much. We found ourselves gasping for air and our heart rates jumped very quickly, around the 140 mark. Bernie's resting heart rate is usually about 50, but at this elevation, it was 65. The next day we cycled to the lunch truck, about 60km, and decided to hitch a ride to our next campsite, giving our bodies another rest. A number of other riders were keeping company with us.

The day we cycled the Blue Nile Gorge was something else, I admire the cyclists who cycled the 18km down AND the 22km up. Bernie and I cycled down and it was exciting to say the least; about half was pavement, but the rest was gravel so we had to take it easy. Before we left, I checked my brakes several times, even though Bernie told me they were fine; one has to be totally responsible for their safety. The ascent was hot, not a breath of air, no shade as we found ourselves struggling around switchbacks like the one in the previous picture, beautiful, but a challenge, to say the least.

Around the 6km mark uphill, with the sweat pouring off our foreheads, guess what greeted us – the common housefly; must have followed us from Canada and because we hadn't seen a shower for a few days, they clung to us as if we were flystickers. We just could not get rid of them, moving so slowly, constantly swatting the pests. We heard the tour truck grinding its way up the hill behind us and it was easy to make a decision – gave the thumbs down, jumped on the truck and got rid of the hills and the flies. That evening a bunch of us walked up to the edge of the gorge and one of our fellow cyclists, Nico, had a bottle of local "hooch"; we sat and watched an amazing sunset over the Blue Nile Gorge while toasting our day.

That evening we stayed at a CPAR (Canadian Physicians for AIDS Relief) camp, which was very accommodating and private; no hordes of kids. We always have to mention the toilets; that was the talk around the campsite usually every evening – you go back to basics very quickly in this environment. At this camp, we couldn't complain; and hamburgers for dinner to boot; what more could one wish for, I ask you.

The next day we felt much stronger and found that with each day, our bodies were getting used to the elevation, so we cycled the whole day, 91km – the hills were bearable. We reached the maximum elevation that we would attain on the tour; 3,122 meters above sea level, in fact the maximum elevation we ever attained on our bikes in our life, considering that PEI's maximum elevation is less than 150 meters. The final day into Addis Ababa, we cycled to the lunch truck, then, having had enough of this high elevation, enjoyed a ride into the capital city, which is situated at an elevation of 2,800 plus meters, thus avoiding riding in a convoy into the heart of the city.

Addis Ababa is a huge city (population of about 3 million) and is the third highest capital city in the world next to La Paz and Quito. We camped on the hotel grounds, figuring our tent was a tad better than the hotel rooms. After setting up our tent on the edge of the hotel courtyard, we set out to see some of the city on foot. When we returned about two hours later, I entered our tent and found that it had been invaded by ants; biting, stinging ants everywhere; they were all over me. Down came the tent and we searched for another spot, which proved to be OK.

We decided to try the hotel restaurant for our evening meal. It was like being back in the 20's (or earlier), with the cashier sitting in the corner cage where you ordered and paid for your drinks and food. He prepared a receipt – two copies – you then proceeded to the bar with your copy. The bartender often went back to the cashier (about 50 feet away) to confirm the order. I ordered a "nice" Ethiopian red wine called Gondar, and at $5.50 a bottle, it was considered expensive; compared to a beer at $0.90, it was. Bernie said that I would have to get used to beer, that our budget might not be able to handle much more of this high-priced wine. No single malt scotch, so it's beer for him. But really, since he left Cairo, he has only had about ten beers in total in a six-week period and five of them were at the Ethiopian border.

I mentioned that riders had been falling ill along the roads through Sudan and Ethiopia, and so far, I had been exempt from that; a few falls, but nothing serious — well that came to an end our first night in Addis Ababa. I caught that same bug and was up to the bathroom three times during the night with both ends working, so I felt pretty awful the first morning in our tent on the hotel grounds. The sun was beating down and I moved my mattress out of the tent and lay down under a nearby tree, but soon lost the shade. We gave up and checked into the hotel, as I could not see myself lying in the sun with absolutely no energy. We brought along our sleeping pads, because they were a tad better than the one in the $12 a night room, where we also shared a bathroom. I lay in bed for the next 24 hours.

One of Bernie's favourite restaurants in Addis Ababa was the Ethio Millenium. Just as an offside, Ethiopia celebrated its millennium in 2008 and there were numerous signs displayed in the city indicating so. The restaurant was very clean, good food, wonderful coffee where he could sip on his cappuccino while waiting for access to the slow dial-up internet. Bernie guessed that some aggressive IT consultants were able to convince the Ethiopian government to beware of the Y2K bug — if there were any problems; it certainly wouldn't have slowed down the internet. It was reported that some people were afraid to ride their donkeys on January 1 — why, he's not sure. Bernie enjoyed the sights of Addis as I continued to nurse my stomach problems.

A number of people on the tour stopped by the barber while resting in Addis and Bernie was among them — got his hair almost completely shaved off — down to about ¼ inch — the shortest he has ever had it in his life. When I saw him coming back from the barber, I thought, what the hell, I'm going to take the plunge too, so I had the barber use one of those hair clippers I had only seen used on men, and she drove it all over my head, about ½ inch from my scalp. Really, I was interested in the convenience of it all, all vanity left me — couldn't see myself anyway — hair grows back. After 24 hours in the hotel room out of the hot sun I was feeling much better and thought a new hair-do would cheer me up.

We departed Addis Ababa in a convoy and I decided to sit on the truck for the morning as when I am cycling in a convoy, I see myself as an accident waiting to happen, possibly taking out a few riders, so better for everyone if I am not there and I don't mind watching from the truck. Besides, I thought I would take it easy on the first day after my stomach sickness.

While sitting on the truck, I noticed that the city streets have a number of large holes on the sides of their streets – not potholes – sewer holes, about two feet square in size. They are completely open – no grates – I am sure people must have fallen into these holes. I didn't see too many tourists walking the streets – wonder why? I was surprised to see the Ethiopian women cleaning the city streets – working with brooms and shovels in the drainage ditches.

Once the convoy reached the outskirts of the city, I joined the cyclists and rode with them to our next campsite.

Ethiopia is a beautiful country – the terrain is mountainous, not rugged, just old mountains, many of which are cultivated in patchwork-like farms. There are villages everywhere – even on top of the mountains, very picturesque. They grow wheat everywhere – you would think they would be more progressive with the growing seasons and the amount of arable land they have. Many trees have been cut down over the centuries for firewood and housing material, with little or no reforestation plan.

Bernie and I get off to an early start this morning cycling through the countryside, through many villages, dodging kids and cows. This part of Ethiopia is heavily populated in the rural areas and the towns are full of people – a very young population. As mentioned, most people use their homes only for shelter; they spend their daylight hours outdoors where their village street is their home. As a result, the streets are filled with people when we pass through – something like our hometown village of North Rustico on Canada Day at parade time – no kidding. Oh yes, we usually have to negotiate cattle as well. I have not seen any fences since leaving Cairo; the cattle are kept by herdsmen and we have dodged by a number of herds along the way.

My thoughts were driven back to my childhood on the family farm on Prince Edward Island while cycling through the Ethiopian countryside. The pictures above brought back memories, and this particular story is directed to my brothers who all worked on the farm with my Dad (sometimes I was allowed to work in the fields with them). You guys may have thought you had it rough in the 50s and 60s having to thresh the grain every summer. I'm sure the system they have here in Ethiopia hasn't changed since wheat was first grown, wheat being one of their main crops. They begin by tilling the soil by oxen and plow (the plow is made from a tree trunk with a blade attached to the end of it to dig into the earth). They plant the wheat by hand, cut it by hand, and carry it in bundles to various areas of the field in big piles. They use cattle to walk in a small circle to separate the wheat from the stalks, which takes days to complete. Once the wheat is separated from the stalks, they then have to separate it from the chaff. Usually you will see the women on the side of the road on a windy day throwing the wheat and chaff up in the air – the wind blows the chaff and the wheat falls to the ground. It is now ready for sale or barter. The previous pictures tell the story.

A Terrifying Experience

Mid-morning on the second day out of Addis Ababa, when I was finally back to my old self and feeling much better, I found myself cycling ahead of Bernie and negotiating my passage through one of the many Ethiopian villages, one similar to the picture above; people everywhere. Usually you can pick your path and move through at about 10-15 kph. I was cycling about that speed and had a good six-foot-wide clear path to take me though a corridor of people and cattle on both sides of the street.

Suddenly, about twelve feet ahead of me, a little girl, about 3 years old, darted across my path; I had no chance. I applied both front and back brakes and slowed down enough so as not to injure the child – I knocked her down with my front wheel and because I braked so suddenly, the momentum of the force of the bike shifted to my body and while falling on my right knee and elbow, I jammed myself into the pitted pavement. I managed to fall in the opposite direction of the child, thus sparing her from injury. The fact that I got hurt was nothing – what ensued after was a nightmare.

When I fell, the townspeople gathered around and were very kind – some even helping me back on my feet. Bernie was on the scene quickly. The little girl was shaken up but not hurt, as my front wheel had hit her from the rear and I had fallen in the opposite direction. She was sitting on the road with her mother, crying, with no open wounds – a blessing. Bernie was attending to my cuts with the small supply of first aid bandages we carried. We were on the scene about ten minutes when two fellow cyclists came by – one went back to get help from the sweep, (a crewmember cycling in last position), and the other went forward to get help from the tour operators. Fortunately, Luke, our tour doctor, was cycling that day, luckily behind us, and came on the scene about 20 minutes after my fall. With Doctor Luke on site, I was in good hands; allowing Bernie to step aside ensuring our bikes and bags were safe. By that time, the little girl and her mother had left the scene.

Duncan, our tour leader, also happened to be cycling that day and caught up to us. A truck was radioed and we stood in the crowd waiting for it to arrive. In the meantime, the crowd was getting larger and larger. Bernie quietly mentioned to me that we could possibly give the mother some money for the mishap, and I nodded my approval; only he and I shared that. As I said, the crowd was very friendly at first, but things changed as time passed. We noticed that about twenty to thirty men had gathered (ages about 20 to 50); one man came forward and demanded that we pay 300 Birr – Ethiopian currency (about $30), because he claimed the child was in the hospital and needed the money. Thirty dollars is not a great amount of money. We could have given it to him at that moment, but we knew that the next guy in our path would demand the same or more and it would just go on and on. Doctor Luke then spoke up and asked to see the child; we knew she was not hurt and that this was just a ploy. We kept asking to see the child and they just kept asking for the money.

A local driver in a truck drove up. He stopped and was asked if he would transport me to the lunch truck, about 30km ahead, which he agreed to do. I got in the truck, but the crowd would not let us leave the scene. They stopped the driver by blocking the wheels with large rocks and after much shouting and yelling, it was decided that I was to get out of the truck and the driver drove on alone.

When our tour truck arrived, I immediately got in and felt relieved and much safer. When our driver started to drive on to the lunch truck with Doctor Luke accompanying us to attend to my wounds, the men again suddenly circled the vehicle – not letting us move forward or backward. Some of the men were holding big rocks ready to throw at the vehicle if we moved. Not once, did I look at any of those men in the eye; rather, I just sat in the vehicle looking over the crowd, not uttering a word. I thought it best that I stay out of it, I felt that the tour operators were dealing with the situation as best they could; my voice would just have exacerbated the situation. In the meantime, Duncan and Doctor Luke were trying to negotiate with the men who were shouting and yelling, demanding money because of the mishap. The police were eventually called to the scene. We managed to move forward and the truck ran over a rock that someone had put under the wheel – I immediately thought that we had ran over a child – seriously, I was scared at this point. We then managed to back up and turn around very quickly and we were on our way to the lunch truck with the doctor. Duncan remained at the site negotiating with the police; I was very concerned for his safety.

We rode about 6km down the road, when a police officer caught up to us on a motorcycle and stopped us, insisting we return to the scene where they wanted me to remain – you might say, for ransom. After much discussion and shouting, we had no alternative but to turn back. In the meantime, Henry Gold, the owner of Tour d'Afrique had arrived on the scene, and he stepped in to negotiate with the police. I was driven to the police station and was relieved at being able to remain in the tour vehicle; as Henry spoke on my behalf. The police asked for my name, which I wrote on a piece of paper and handed it to Henry to give to the police. The mother brought the child to the station and we saw that the little girl was OK. Henry asked the mother how much money she wanted for the inconvenience, she replied, "100 Birr", ($10). She was given the money and we were on our way.

Of course, we could have used this occasion to give this family a great deal more money, but the mob took over and I'm sure that would have not been a wise decision.

I have reflected on what happened many times since – I was really scared someone would be hurt or even killed. The angry faces on those men and the shouting and yelling that took place between the tour operators, locals, and the police was very disturbing. Resting on the shoulder of one man was a steel bar about 3 inches wide, 2 feet long, and about one-half inch thick. I was afraid that one of the tour operators was going to get that across his back. I was worried for Bernie who had left the scene on bike, accompanied by a tour support person; and was also worried for all the other riders who were cycling behind me. Fortunately, there were no further incidents relating to this story.

What we really faced was a situation that escalated because of language problems, too much testosterone, and no doubt, poverty. There was an older woman sitting on the ground in the crowd moaning and moving her hands all over her face and arms indicating that the child was bleeding, when in fact, there was not a scratch on her – that is how things had escalated and rumours had spread. I'm sure some of the townspeople might have heard that the child had died. In hindsight, maybe we should have gotten out of there as soon as I could manage to get back on my bike, or better still, have gone to the police. However, we were concerned about the child and did not want to just take off. I will always be grateful to Duncan, Doctor Luke, and Henry Gold for looking after me; their careful negotiations got us through this terrifying situation unharmed. Henry Gold does not always accompany the tour; it was my luck to have him with us at this time. The whole incident took approximately three hours, although it seemed much, much longer.

If I look at it from the eyes of the locals, they saw me knocking down a child in their town, and within 20 minutes, I am looked after by a doctor and have all the care that can be provided, given the circumstances. And they have very little, if anything; really poor, so they do the only thing they can think of at the time and that is to demand money. It was extortion, but they had nothing to lose and saw an opportunity to get some money from the foreigners. You will not see any pictures of this incident; that was the last thing on our minds during this very terrifying time.

That evening at camp, I received excellent care from Doctor Luke and Nurse Amadine, requiring eight stitches in my knee and two in my elbow, which kept me off my bike for the next four days. In trying to keep the atmosphere around the campsite somewhat light after the fear we had experienced, we joked while sitting around – I wasn't worth too much – only a $10 ransom. We had to keep things in perspective throughout the trip, which is what kept us going. Of course, the next rest day, the tour operators were treated to a cold beer on us.

While the tour operators were dealing with my situation, another was occurring a few kilometers ahead of us. A rider had stopped to take some pictures in the countryside and a local man came up to her, pushed her down, stole her camera, and ran off. Fortunately, some other locals saw what was happening and chased the guy down, retrieved the camera and brought it back to her.

For the next two weeks or so, I could not stop thinking that as I had given my name to the police; I would be stopped at the border crossing and held until I gave them more money. I would then tell myself that this was anxious thinking on my part and maybe I was becoming a little paranoid. I kept these thoughts to myself, didn't even mention them to Bernie. I need not have worried; the border crossing went smoothly.

The day following my accident, Bernie joined me on the truck; remember, in sickness and in health. Our truck was the last one to leave the campsite and we witnessed something unexpected. As mentioned, Tour d'Afrique prides themselves on not leaving a footprint along our route and especially in our campsites. We bury all compostable waste, burn all non-compostable waste, and leave any empty containers to the village people along with any leftover foodstuffs. That morning, Bernie and I were sitting on the truck and watching the crew prepare for departure. All recyclable materials were left behind in plastic bags for the those waiting for the trucks to leave; probably about 15 or 20 individuals, all ages. As soon as we started moving out, these individuals suddenly went into a frantic mode, grabbing cartons, cans, and bottles from each other, fighting for peanut butter, ketchup, and jam bottles, tuna fish and bean cans. It was as if it was gold to them – we took a video of this while driving off into the distance. We have seen stories like this on television from developing countries and we sometimes tend not to totally believe it, as it sometimes seems as if incidents like this must be exaggerated or staged. We saw this with our own eyes and it was very real.

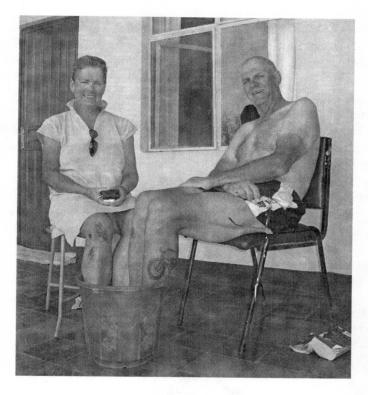

Four days after my accident, we found ourselves on a rest day in a town called Arba Minch, where we were lucky enough to relax in a room. I particularly appreciated this, as it meant that I didn't have to crawl in and out of the tent; a chore with my wounded knee and elbow. I healed very quickly, mainly because of the very dry climate, and having my stitches removed; I was back on my bike after our rest day. This picture shows off my wounds; I call it my "African tattoo", notice Bernie's tattoo of his first bike. Also, notice our slick haircuts we got while in Addis Ababa. Here we are having an African-style footbath outside our motel room.

On this rest day in Arba Minch, we went for a long walk into the town, and while mingling among the people, a young guy, aged 16 or so, latched onto us, asking us if he could help in any way. We mentioned that we were on our way to a bank, as we needed to exchange some money. He offered his assistance in getting us to a bank, something we did not need. Bernie told him up front – "You can walk with us, but I'm telling you right now, we are not paying you for this." He assured us that he did not want any money for his help, but was just interested in being courteous to tourists. He walked along with us, talking incessantly about trying to get an education; a very personable and rather likeable young man. We arrived at the bank and I could go on for the next two pages, but don't want to bore you. It took us about half an hour just to exchange a few US dollars into Ethiopian currency – we went from one clerk to another, giving identification each time; you would have thought we were there to exchange millions. The young lad stuck with us through all this, standing by our side; at times, we were completely ignoring him. He walked out of the bank with us and said, "Where do you want to go now?" At that moment, Bernie says, "OK, we have no further need for your assistance, please just leave us alone." No such luck – he stuck to us like the housefly going up the Blue Nile Gorge a week or so ago. We didn't want to cause a scene, so we relented and gave him probably the equivalent of one dollar to get rid of him. They know they are going to win when they latch on to tourists, as we are not going to cause a commotion when trying to say good-bye to them. There is very little work for these young people in the bigger towns, so they invent their own jobs.

On our way back to the campsite, we stopped by a school where we visited with students who were outside enjoying their recess. It was a private school, very well behaved children, all dressed in uniforms. We spoke to the schoolmaster, who was most interested in telling us all about the school and letting us know about the shortages they were experiencing – the conversation was very interesting. They are so dependent on donations.

As we take off from Arba Minch, as it happened, it was Bernie's day to break the routine – the story goes like this – in his own words.

We had four remaining cycling days before reaching the Kenyan border and because this was Beryl's first day cycling since her accident, she decided to cycle just to the lunch truck, about 65km. After lunch, I was feeling great, rather frisky now that my legs were in pretty good shape and I knew that Beryl was feeling better; she was to spend the second half of her day on the truck. I surprised myself; I was able to keep pace with the "young folk". When inquiring about Beryl, I told them "she released me, eat my dust", but they would always catch me in a few kilometers, and I would tell them that I slowed down to enjoy the scenery; yeah, right.

The route instructions for that day were to keep left at the roundabout in Konso (82km mark on my odometer) and then take the road on the right after 2 kilometers. Well I thought it was after the 92km mark on my odometer. It was great cycling on a downhill dirt road where I was doing 40-45km/h, "in the zone" as they say, thinking I had eight or so more kilometers to the turn off. Well I missed the ribbon markers, but continued to follow bicycle tracks, which confirmed in my mind that I was going in the right direction, as the visible tracks that were there would have been made by our cyclists. Many bicycle tracks are erased by passing vehicles, but often the smoothest, or more accurately, the less-bumpy section of the road was near the ditch where tracks usually remained, as was the case on this day. Besides, this was an extremely poor part of Ethiopia and local cyclists were rare, which further convinced me that the tracks were made by one of our cyclists.

About four kilometers past the turn-off, I heard someone shouting my name (I am easily recognized in the village of North Rustico, but here in Ethiopia, nah). Well it could have been a superior being telling me that I was lost, but no, it was a very winded, non-smiling Doctor Luke, who shouted to me "You took the wrong road". "Who, me"? It was an unexpected, unpleasant 4km climb back to the correct route. Of course, I was eternally grateful to Doctor Luke, and sharing a cold beer with him at the next rest stop was the least I could do.

Back at the camp, Doctor Luke told me that fortunately he caught a glimpse of me missing the turnoff and took four kilometers to catch me as I was "moving". I later discovered that the tracks I followed were those of a fellow lost rider who was told by a local truck driver that he had missed the turn-off. Incidentally, when cycling through towns, especially with roundabouts, we would often hesitate on which exit to take, but the locals would give us directions, which were always correct, no practical jokers.

On that same afternoon, about three kilometers from the bush camp, I came on a group of our younger cyclists, one of whom had a tire puncture. I stopped, but no assistance was required and by that time there were eight or ten kids, mostly boys aged 10 to 12 years, gathered around. I asked them if I could take their picture; of course they agreed and were excited, especially when they saw their images on the small LCD screen. I always kept coins and indicated that I would give them each a coin for allowing me to photograph them. When I opened my bike bag to get the coins, I was mobbed and almost pushed down. A couple of our cyclists literally pulled them off me. These kids were extremely poor; most would rarely have earned or received money. I tried to get them to line up to give them each a coin, but alas, as I gave a coin to one, he would simple push his way back to me. Solution, when placing a coin in a hand, I would grab his arm and whip him aside. Believe it or not, they quickly got the message and order was restored. With beaming smiles, they all high-fived me when I departed, and the memories are priceless.

While cycling in the southern part of Ethiopia, it seemed like the Ethiopians had developed a new way of farming – we saw termite mounds everywhere, as far as the eye could see, quite stunning actually. All different sizes and shapes made out of the beautiful iron-rich red earth – almost as if they had been carefully planted.

During the last few days in Ethiopia, we noticed a greater number of cattle being herded to market; we later learned that Ethiopia has the largest livestock population in Africa. The village of Dubluck in southern Ethiopia has one of the biggest livestock markets in East Africa, and we were told that animals trek for days, before being trucked off to the Middle East or fattened up for butchers in Ethiopia, Kenya, and Uganda.

We found ourselves weaving in and out among the cattle with little thought of being gored by one of their huge horns, because these cattle are very docile. What Bernie didn't expect, when he met a boy about 10 years of age herding cattle and accompanied by two adults, was to be whacked on the back by the boy's prodding stick after passing him. Boys walking with an adult never seem to throw stones and often don't even beg. However, I suppose this lad saw an opportunity. Bernie dropped his bike and gave chase, but knew that it was no use; the boy was already 100 meters off into the distance, another future Olympian no doubt. The adults seem to gesture an apology, which was accepted; no great harm was done, thanks to Bernie's camelback (water container) that took a direct hit.

Among these termite-infested areas and more toward the Kenyan border, we entered some very poor villages – we hadn't thought that things could actually become poorer. The huts deteriorated until they looked like those in the above picture. There is no lack of thorns in Africa and the villagers make use of them by fashioning a fence around their huts to keep animals from roaming through their grounds. There are absolutely no amenities to be seen – basic sustenance in a very dry land. We did see many NGO signs along the way, where non-governmental organizations from around the world are helping these impoverished people. NGOs like WaterCan, our charity, for whom we have been raising funds to help dig wells for the rural people, are busy and their efforts can be seen in Ethiopia, Kenya, Uganda, and Tanzania. As I cycled through these very poor villages, memories of my school days came back to me; we would have "penny drives" for the people in Africa. Even back in the 50s and 60s, we learned about the plight of the poor people in Africa.

I am proud to tell you that the last day of cycling before we reached the Kenyan border, I cycled the whole day, after the past four days of cycling just half-days. This was the first full day of cycling since my accident, and it was particularly satisfying to give a thumbs-up when the tour truck passed me.

I want to share some of my feelings with you as to how I felt at this time on the tour now that I have had time to reflect. I often speak of living in the now, and I will try to describe just how I realized that I no longer found myself thinking about the past or future. As you have read, the first two months – riding through Egypt, Sudan, and Ethiopia – were the toughest days of the tour for most riders. Psychologically, it was great to get the toughest part of the tour over with, knowing that things would pick up as we made our way to the south of the continent. Each night while preparing for a night's sleep, I was so at peace, with Bernie lying next to me. It seemed that I was in 'heaven' in the wilds of the deserts of Northern Africa enjoying the rest and the silence – no TV, no household or work duties or bills to attend to, no internet; just the beautiful sky filled with stars; you'll not find too many clouds in the skies over the deserts. I asked myself why I should be so happy in these surroundings after so many days on the bike, riding solo, as Bernie and I did not cycle together – we were usually about 100 meters apart from each other. I think part of the answer lies in the fact that I found myself only thinking in the now – it was very spiritual, cycling through the deserts where the Bible stories came alive – it was as if I was reliving the stories I had heard in my childhood. What made it so authentic was that the people, who live in the rural areas, still live as in the times of the Bible, or it seemed so, but it is their present.

Possibly another reason I was so happy was that I had been living outdoors in the fresh air for the past two months in total sunshine. No short days like we experience in Canada during the winter months. Of course, Bernie was just as happy as I was, thus adding to my happiness. I've never considered myself a very spiritual person, but I later found cycling was awakening something within me, and I didn't realize this until some months later back in Canada which probably motivated me to write this book.

Being on a tour of this nature with tour operators meant that we were looked after like children – we were told when to rise in the morning, break down our tents, eat breakfast, hop on our bikes, and take off for the day, stopping for lunch – then off to the next campsite for dinner. All meals prepared for us, no need to worry about grocery shopping. The above picture shows one of our three tour vehicles, which carried all our equipment. The tour operators planned our route; we didn't have to think about anything – except getting from point A to point B each day. We were like 12-year-olds and most 12-year-olds are pretty happy. The daily grind and routine provided us with a sense of security, much like a 4-year-old wanting to watch their favourite movie over and over again. The tour so far had also given me the opportunity to get to know myself again, the old Beryl Buote from Rusticoville, P.E.I.

LALIBELLA – ZANZIBAR – SERENGETI

An Unscheduled Tour – Without Bicycles!

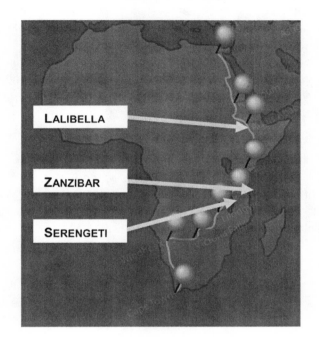

Entry: February 29, 2008   Exit: March 12, 2008

DUE TO UNREST IN KENYA DURING THIS PERIOD IN 2008, THE TOUR OPERATORS made a decision not to take us through the country and alternate plans were made. We were disappointed when we first learned that we would not be cycling through Kenya and, more importantly, it all seemed so unreal that we would not be cycling for the next two weeks. Members of the group formed smaller groups and planned their two weeks off. One group planned to climb Mount Kilimanjaro, Tanzania's highest peak, this option was out for Bernie and I; we did not give it a thought.

The trucks, carrying all our equipment including our bikes, made their way through Kenya safely to Arusha, Tanzania, where all riders were to meet to resume the tour on March 12.

Lalibella's Christian Churches

We took a tour bus back to Addis Ababa from the Kenyan border and Bernie and I, along with some fellow riders, hopped on a flight to Lalibella, just north of Addis Ababa. Lalibella is famous for its eleven Christian churches, carved out of rock in the Area Mountains during the 12th century. The process is underway to get this site classified as the Eighth Wonder of the World.

Each of the churches in Lalibella, which were built by King Lalibella, is quite unique. Up until the time of the 12th century AD, some Ethiopian Christians would make a pilgrimage to Jerusalem and Bethlehem once in their lifetime, similar to the Muslims going to Mecca and the Hindus going to the Ganges River. At that time, the Ethiopian Christians had to travel through Sudan and the Northern African nations populated mostly by Muslim Arabs, and very often, these Christians had to venture into unfriendly territory. King Lalibella decided to create an attraction to allow Ethiopians to stay within their own country while making a pilgrimage to these stone churches. Each of the churches was named after a saint or angel, taking a quarter of a century to complete, using about 4,000 workers. There is a myth that after a day of chiseling, each night the angels would do three times the work the men had done during the day, but it still took a quarter of a century to finish (I bet those angels were all female). Those days, you didn't work thirteen weeks to get your hours for EI (employment insurance); you just worked week-in, week-out, for years.

A cross was designed for each of the churches. These crosses are unique and symbolic – they measure about 12 inches in length – some are made of pure gold, but many, like this one, are made of brass. The churches are still used today by the more than 18,000 people in the village. So 11 churches for 18,000 people and there is no plan to close any of them. Lots of monks, I suppose. When we took a picture of the monks with their crosses, we asked their permission first; they would then put on their sunglasses to protect their eyes. There was a basket at the door for us to drop a donation.

For the first time in our lives, we went to church 'several times' on the same Sunday. Each time we entered a church, we had to remove our shoes and hats. In addition to our guide, Mario, we had a "shoeman" who looked after our shoes and if we exited a different door, the shoeman carried our shoes to our exit door and had them all lined up for us. Very often, there were pesky flies buzzing around us and we were given a small branch from a pepper tree to swat these flies. Bernie warned us not to say, "Shoo, man, those flies are pesky!", so as not to offend the shoeman. At the end of the day, it was customary for everyone to give the shoeman a tip for his services.

It was a very quiet and spiritual experience and no doubt, Lalibella will become one of the Wonders of the World. Bernie and I got to walk through the 'eye of the needle', shown in this photograph. As it is said in the Bible; "It is easier for a camel to walk through the eye of a needle than for a rich man to enter the Kingdom of Heaven"; we breezed through the eye of the needle, have no money, and now are working on our journey to Heaven.

When we walked through the touristy town of Lalibella, we were joined by young people about high-school age asking for money so they could buy school material. They would catch us exiting an internet café, knowing that we would have an email address, asking us for our co-ordinates, latching onto us as if we were their adoptive parents.

We spent over three weeks in Ethiopia, a beautiful country with amazing scenery. Of all the countries we visited in Africa on the complete tour, the women and children of Ethiopia will fondly remain in my thoughts. I have enjoyed sharing some of those memories with you.

The Isle of Zanzibar

From Lalibella, we took a flight to the Island of Zanzibar, off the east coast of Tanzania, very touristy with lovely beaches. We don't have to work on our tans; we are sometimes mistaken for locals; even so, we planned on lying on the beach and hope to take in some snorkeling.

We spent two days in Zanzibar Town, the main city, situated on the southwest coast of the Island. We stayed in "Stone Town", the old section of Zanzibar Town, at a quaint little hotel. Bernie had to be ever so careful, because the door to our room was a "split" door with a bolt and padlock, much like you'd find on a ship so he had to remember to bend down while entering the room. The windows in the room didn't have glass, just screens, and the call to prayer at 4:00 a.m. made it seem like the mosque was next door. In case you didn't wake up with the call to prayer, the roosters ensured you didn't sleep in too late.

We enjoyed fine cappuccino – and ice cream – something we had not tasted for two months; and of course, Bernie found a restaurant serving Stella Artois beer. We spent our time walking in and out of boutiques, negotiating the narrow streets, and were met by the ever-present street vendors who sell t-shirts, sunglasses, and cashew nuts. Although Bernie ate his cashew nuts, he still has his sunglasses and t-shirt, another tiring day of bartering.

In many parts of Africa, we experienced scheduled power shutdowns while visiting the towns and cities across the continent and the Town of Zanzibar was not spared. We had visited an internet café before the shutdown and successfully used the system at the going hourly rate. During the shutdown, we heard that this particular café had a power generator and all was working well. As there was limited things to do during the shutdown, we thought, well why not try to get in touch with friends and family again. We entered the café and were surprised to hear that the hourly rate had just doubled. We expected to see a small increase, but double the rate – the owner commented that he was 'the only show in town'.

After spending two days in Stone Town, we, along with seven members of our group hired a van and were driven to the northern tip of the Island, about 65km. Most of us settled on a mid-priced resort ranging from $50 to $90 per night. The $50 rate got you a nice room, but without air-conditioning; $70 included air-conditioning; and $90 included an ocean view and the sound of the waves lapping on the beach. Our budget only allowed us an air-conditioned unit, so we had to forego an ocean view. Bernie wanted me to get a large pail of water, sit outside the door of our room, and slosh the water back and forth to replicate the surf while he looked at a picture of the beach on our laptop, but there is a limit to what I will do to keep him happy. We compromised and sat in the beach bar and watched the amazing sunset – a rival to our sunset over beautiful Cavendish Beach back home on Prince Edward Island.

We booked a snorkeling trip on a 30-foot wooden boat, about the size of the Sea Queen III, but with a 40-horsepower motor. The Sea Queen would have left us in her wake (the Sea Queen belongs to one of Bernie's friends in North Rustico, Prince Edward Island). We sailed about two hours to an island reef where we anchored in about 15 feet of water and snorkeled for about two hours. The scenes were breathtaking – large schools of fish. We had lunch on the boat; barbecued king mackerel and local fruit. After lunch, we snorkeled without our fins. The small zebra fish, about three inches in length, liked to nibble on the calluses on our feet, so we got a free pedicure to boot.

The Wilds of the Serengeti

Tanzania contains many large and ecologically significant wildlife parks including the famous Serengeti National Park and the Ngorongoro Crater in the north, the Selous Game Reserve and Mikumi National Park in the south. Gombe National Park in the west is known as the site of Doctor Jane Goodall's studies of chimpanzee behavior.

If you ever have the opportunity of travelling to this country, don't miss visiting the Serengeti and the Ngorongoro Crater – it is 'a must'. We spent a day and a half in the Plaines of the Serengeti and a half-day sightseeing in the Crater.

We set out from camp with about 20 fellow riders in three land cruisers (six to eight of us in each vehicle). On our way to the park, one of the cruisers (not ours) had an accident. The driver decided to stop to allow his guests to take some pictures of giraffes who were about to cross the road. He pulled over to the side of the road and backed over a drainage culvert, and the van tipped over on its side; thankfully, no one was injured. By the way, it was the only culvert for miles, what were the odds of backing over it.

It took about two hours to get the vehicle out of the ditch, another sideshow we hadn't expected. Then suddenly out of nowhere – a family of giraffes made their way across the highway in perfect unison. We arrived at the park about 3:00 p.m., stunned at the amount of wildlife we saw along the way.

The park is extremely beautiful in its completely natural setting – the animals have free range, therefore you will not see a sign indicating what animals we are approaching, as they move around a lot. We were not allowed to get out of the vehicles, mostly because you never know when a lion could be stalking a grazing animal. The animals are familiar with the land cruisers, so we could get very close to most of them, as evidenced by our photos, see our website, www.rusticoriders.ca, and follow the link.

The Flats of the Ngorongoro Crater

Riding through the crater, we were again among many animals, much the same as in the Serengeti Park. While on route to the crater, we stopped to visit the Old Duvai Gorge Museum, founded by Mary Leakey in the late 1970s. A number of our group decided to drop in and view an exhibit dedicated to the Latoli fossilized footprints. While waiting for some members of our tour, I walked off-site a short distance and Bernie stayed behind chatting with fellow cyclists. While gazing at the countryside, I was approached by a young Masai mother holding her baby, who appeared to be very sick and feeble, runny nose and all. She motioned that she wanted me to buy one of her bracelets and immediately put it on my arm. I was suddenly swarmed by eight or ten other women, all wanting me to purchase bracelets from each of them. After placing their bracelets on each of my arms – I must have had ten or so draped on each arm. I shouted "No", and began taking all the bracelets off except for the one the first girl put on. I then gave her the equivalent of $5. and walked away from the group. I thought it was a good occasion to give this person some money, as we had not been too generous to many people while cycling, especially in Ethiopia, for fear of being swarmed by children and adults alike. I then jumped on the land cruiser to avoid being harassed by more people. A man approached me as I sat on the truck, holding a baby on his shoulder, obviously wanting money. I then noticed that he was holding the same sick child that belonged to the Masai woman to whom I gave money. I felt somewhat cheated, but wrote it off to another experience.

Later on that evening, while camping a few hundred meters from the edge of the Ngorongoro Crater and after a magnificent day of sightseeing, a number of us from our group were milling about our campsite when a huge bull elephant walked by, less than 100 meters from us. At that moment, we noticed a fellow cyclist approaching the bull with his camera and got a bit too close and suddenly, the bull charged. I never saw a cyclist move so quickly without his bicycle. Apparently, it was a mock charge; our guide later told us that when an elephant charges with his/her trunk sticking up in the air, this indicates a mock charge. A trunk that is curled between the legs, well, then he means business. Of course, no picture to share.

I cannot fully describe our time spent in the Serengeti and the Crater – pictures describe it best. We were fortunate to have the time to visit the park – a once-in-a-lifetime opportunity. This one evening in our tent, we shared the grounds with zebras and elephants, which were not too far off and kept in line by the park rangers.

The Serengeti and the Crater are great examples of a very green environment – nothing has been touched – dirt roads still abound, there are no power lines. We rode by various species of animals, including, naming just a few: elephants, giraffes, zebras, hippos, gazelles, lions, warthogs, hyenas, topis, impala, wildebeest, rhinos, monkeys, and birds of all kinds. These animals live in the wild looking after their own species without the interference of humans. We found ourselves so quiet and peaceful when stopping to observe a family of lions having an afternoon siesta on the open plains. Decades ago, poaching of animals was a big problem, and in some areas it still is; however, Tanzania has really stepped up to the plate and is protecting its parks thus sharing this wonderful resource with the rest of the world.

TANZANIA — OH, THE GREENERY!

Rain – Rain – Rain!

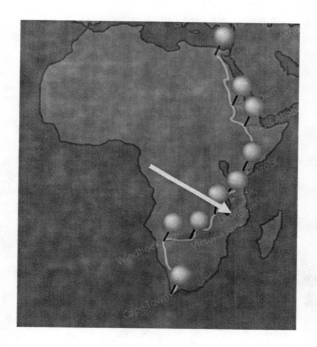

Entry: March 12, 2008 Exit: March 27, 2008	
Rough Roads (clay/washboard/sandy – (km)	503
Pavement – (km)	555
Total Distance – (km)	1,058
Number of Cycling Days	10
Population – millions	38

OUR REST FROM CYCLING THE PAST TWO WEEKS WAS WELL APPRECIATED — cost us a bit, but hey, it is only money. We had forgotten all about the stone-throwing kids of Ethiopia and were looking forward to the beautiful terrain that lay ahead of us. It was great meeting up with all the riders and hearing about their experiences over the past two weeks; from climbing Mount Kilimanjaro, travelling through Uganda and Rwanda, to going on park safaris. A few of the riders enjoyed a complete rest for the two-week period and set up camp in Arusha, Tanzania, where we all met to resume our tour.

Until we reached Arusha, we had not seen a drop of rain — cloudless skies all the way. Now we know why Tanzania was so lush; yes, it was their rainy season and we had nightly downpours. Oh well, at least we don't have to shovel it.

For the past two months, we had been cycling on the right hand side of the road as we do in North America; for the next half of the tour, we would have to move to the left hand side of the road. This caused for a little anxiety at first, but we soon got used to it.

After a 2-week rest, we looked forward to seven consecutive cycling days travelling from Arusha to the City of Iringa, our next planned rest day. The first day was 110km of pavement, so everyone reached camp by 2:00 p.m. This camp was equipped with showers and a covered eating area, which came in handy, because we had another early evening rain-shower. This being the first day on the road since our two-week 'vacation', the tour operators went out of their way in preparing a steak dinner where we sat under a thatched-roof picnic area. A sharp contrast from the desert camps in Sudan and Ethiopia.

After setting up our tent, we noticed that very close to where we pitched it, there was a partially covered hole in the ground, the remnants of an old well. While I was breaking down camp the next morning, Bernie decided to make a video – a take-off of Dolores Claiborne, a movie based on the book by Stephen King. While shooting the video he, of course, narrated what was taking place as he walked around with his camera. I have listened to his narration; here is how it goes:

Many have seen the movie 'Dolores Claiborne' – well this is our campsite and right behind our tent is the perfect Dolores Claiborne "get rid of your husband" movie setting. As you can see, it is about a 30-foot deep well. Last evening, Beryl tried to get me to chase her, she was going to jump over the well, and you know what was going to happen to me, and then the insurance policy – I know, and she knows, that I am worth more dead than alive.

I believe Bernie's mind was wandering a bit; thinking that I was trying to get him back for the time I caught him trying to smuggle a bottle of scotch through Sudan in my permanent bag; because, as I told you, if they had searched my bag, I may have been shot.

The next six days of cycling to the City of Iringa were days from hell, especially for me. The roads were just plain dirt – lots of rocks, mud, hills, and thorns. In the beginning, I was just too careful on these roads, moving along rather slowly, but soon realized that you must move along fairly fast, as it takes too much effort to control the bike when you hit rocks while riding slowly. I got the knack of it after awhile but when I got tired, it was easy to lose concentration and that became a set-up for a fall – which *did not* happen.

On the third day, on these roads from hell, I decided to set Bernie free and off he went leaving me behind. My plan was to jump on the last truck, giving Bernie the assurance that I would be OK – another thumbs-down day for me. Therefore, each morning, I would start cycling on those dirt roads while having everything shaken out of me, and then I would jump on the truck. I found out that the trucks moved slower than the cyclists did, because it was so rocky – it was like being on one of those vibration beds that were popular in the traveler motels of the 60s. I mention a week from hell for me, but for Bernie, it was one of his best weeks. He got used to riding "off-road" and could set his own pace without me; he really enjoyed himself. He had one fall, but nothing serious.

We passed through many small villages on our route and were amazed, as always, to see the way the rural people live – again, it doesn't look like anything much has changed in the past century. I did notice that instead of the usual mud roof, some used corrugated steel and put rocks all over the top of it so it didn't blow away. Some even had grass growing on their rooftops. The mud houses are not too high – less than six feet – small windows, no electricity nor running water. Most people were subsistence farmers, growing just enough food to feed themselves and their animals – enough to get by until the next crop. They grow corn, sunflowers, and watermelons all around their mud huts. You will not see Tanzanians spending most of their day cutting grass around these modest homes – no lawnmowers here.

Many Tanzanians wear t-shirts and pants, which have come from the Western world – we even saw a Toronto Maple Leaf jersey – the person wearing it probably didn't know that the team won't make the playoffs again this year – as a matter of fact we are pretty certain that he knew very little about ice hockey.

The baobab tree can be seen all over the central countries through which we travelled. Their huge trunks have the ability to store water, much like a camel who prepares himself for long dry periods in the desert.

We learned that a certain baobab tree situated in Limpopo, South Africa holds a drink bar in its hollowed trunk. The tree stands 72 feet high, with a circumference of 155 feet. The tree has its own cellar with natural ventilation to keep the beer cool. It is so wide it takes 40 adults with outstretched arms to encircle it. Carbon dating has determined that the tree is 6,000 years old. When baobabs are more that 1,000 years old, they hollow out naturally, in this case allowing them to convert the hollow into a pub. The baobab tree, also called the 'tree of life', is capable of providing shelter, food, and water for animals and human inhabitants of the African Savanna. The fruit of the tree is called "monkey bread" and is an important source of vitamin C for many animals. The baobab is a sacred tree in African culture, and has many legends involving it. For example, if anyone picks a baobab flower, he or she would be eaten by a lion. Bernie asked me to pick him a bouquet; fortunately, they were too high to reach. Other legends: if a baby drinks a concoction made from baobab bark, the baby, it is said, will grow up mighty and powerful, and if a person drinks water in which seeds from the tree have been soaked, he will be safe from a crocodile attack. In our case, when we do reach a baobab tree, you can see that it provides a great deal of privacy for off-road toilet duties.

Speaking of toilet duties, again, it is still a nightly topic around the campsite. I think we are all regressing; did we ever think this would be a topic of discussion when signing up for the tour? Bernie's new definition of frustration is the day he had stomach cramps and had to leave camp several times to go dig a hole. Often this is quite a chore, to find a secluded spot with soft ground and no thorns. However, the last time, after walking a fair distance through thorn bushes and watching out for poisonous snakes, he finally found a good spot and dug his hole, crouched, but alas only farted – all that work for nothing, well almost nothing.

After six days on the 'off roads', we are now in the City of Iringa staying at a Baptist Conference Centre where we have a motel room – albeit very basic. We have a TV but no remote, which we don't need anyway, because there is only one station and it's in Swahili. I unplugged the TV to plug my computer into the outlet, and, while doing so, the whole outlet fell apart. Bernie went to the reception desk to tell them that we needed an electrician. It was just too much to expect that an electrician would come to fix our problem, but within ten minutes, he arrived on a motorcycle and fixed the plug in a few seconds – a tip was in order.

The Tanzanian people were very accommodating, to an extent that sometimes surprised us. Since leaving Cairo, hiring taxi drivers, while on rest days, is sometimes a challenge, as when they see a *muzungu* – white person – looking for taxi service, the fare is usually increased substantially and the bartering begins. Much to our surprise, when we hailed a taxi from downtown Iringa to take us back to our campsite, our driver was wearing a suit and tie; the day being Sunday, he had been to church. While chatting, we learned that he was a schoolteacher, very personable, talking about an orphanage he was involved with outside his regular teaching duties. We chatted about a number of topics including our tour. When we arrived at the campsite, he refused to take our fare; Bernie insisted and eventually he accepted the money. This story was a 180-degree shift from most other taxi experiences we had.

Here you see the gardener at the Baptist Conference Centre looking after the grounds. You might think he was swinging a golf club, but he is using a scythe, this particular one has about a six-inch curved blade at the bottom of it that cuts through the grass. Now there's a job that will never end. A good way to condition one's golf swing, they should think of setting up a golf school, a moneymaking offshoot from this chore.

The restaurant facilities were limited at the center; this picture shows the women working in their outdoor kitchen. Again, people don't work indoors too much when the outdoor climate is gentle enough to work all year round.

Bernie spent last evening sitting outside our motel room door with fellow cyclists, acting as the tour guitarist; the locals gathered around – it was a nice time. I enjoyed the music and laughter while tucked away in my bed, yes, a real bed.

Tanzania is a gorgeous country – a lot of red earth like PEI – very lush with many hills. Most rural people don't own cars; they walk everywhere and carry their wood, corn, and watermelons either on their back or on their head – it is really a sight to see. Women and children mostly do the majority of walking and transporting. There are many bicycles on the roads – old bicycles with no gears and many guys walk downhill with their bicycle, as they often don't have brakes. They carry all kinds of items on their bikes; in the previous picture, a coke vendor had just replenished his supply.

It was a treat to be cycling on pavement since leaving Iringa, but Bernie missed the rough roads – I guess the only roads he will cycle from now on are the red roads on PEI. We changed from our knobbie tires back to the road tires – our Schwalbes and, hopefully, no more flats. We hadn't had any flats since leaving Cairo, but eight flats with the knobbies on the rough roads – hurrah for Schwalbes.

It was smooth sailing to the first bush camp after leaving Iringa – we noted that the road repair crews simply laid out tree branches or a line of stones on the road to warn oncoming motorists. No need for a flag person – I suppose those drawing employment insurance have to get their weeks some other way (there is no social programs like that here!). We noticed that the terrain looked very much like PEI – rolling hills, very lush, and again, the red soil.

One of our campsites, while in this rainy season, was in a wooded area with limited space for camping. We were to pitch our tents on the trail in the woods where every tent was set up in a row, as shown in the picture, opposite. In the early evening, we had a torrential downpour and a few tents were washed out. As we were late arriving in camp, rather than carrying our tent about 100 meters down the trail, we instead chose an area a few yards from the truck where we had to tramp down the ground growth before setting up our tent. It proved to be a good spot, as we were not washed out. You can see our clothes hanging on the line behind our tent; I believe I hung our wet clothes out four nights in a row, to no avail – the humidity was so high during this period. You may also notice that I got fancy and made a little step out of tree bark that was lying around – made for a tidy entrance to our tent.

We are in the hills of Tanzania and, what could be worse, I think I have picked up a bug, (turned out to be a parasite; however, I did not realize it for about ten days or so). I don't have the energy I have had all along, and find myself falling ill along with a number of other riders. This means I have to stop often for a rest when I see some shade along the route. At the same time, Bernie is getting stronger, and having to stop and wait for me at the top of most hills is not fun for him. Today, I guess he had had enough of me; when I shouted for him to stop, he did, but when I finally made it to the top of the hill, he said he could not cycle like this anymore and frustratingly threw his bike in the ditch. He picked it up and rode off by himself out of my sight. I rested and got back on my bike, knowing that I would just move along slowly and when the next tour truck came along, jump on and ride to camp. I was cycling at a slow pace, came around a turn in the road, and saw Bernie sitting on the roadside dike waiting for me. When I arrived, he started to cry, feeling bad for his behaviour – we hugged and moved along. I know how he felt and it wasn't fair for me to expect him to be forever waiting for me, but being ever optimistic, I was sure I could shake this stomach problem.

The next morning I felt somewhat OK and decided to cycle to the lunch truck (about 60km), then hitch a ride to camp. Bernie could then cycle in the afternoon at his own pace without having to worry about me. In fact, that very afternoon, Bernie broke his speed record on riding downhill – a whopping 82km per hour. The countryside took on the look of the Canadian Maritime provinces, so expansive and lush and many Canadians had to agree with us that evening as we sat around on our campstools. You were lucky if you got one of the stools; our tour members increased because of a number of sectionals who joined us back in Arusha.

All along our route in Tanzania, we continued to see women working the fields and carrying water on their heads from the wells. We also saw children as young as 8 or 9 years of age carrying large jerry cans of water on their heads – barefooted. The women and children worked the fields with big hoes, digging up the grassy soil (yes, heavy grassy sod), some even with a baby on their back in the heat. You often saw children looking after children, as shown in this picture.

Women and girls work the fields wearing long dresses, but then again, a dress would be a tad bit cooler during the heat of the day. The women and children often had to walk long distances to get water and then return to their village carrying the containers on their heads. In some cases, the children miss school because of having to get their daily supply of water, as their towns are without a water system – also no electricity – just a mud hut with a thatched roof. It is true when they say that one of the natural resources of the whole of Africa is their women; they are the backbone of the continent, especially those living in the rural areas. Many women, if they had a chance, could write a book far more interesting and meaningful than this one – their life story would provide us with a better understanding of their daily plight.

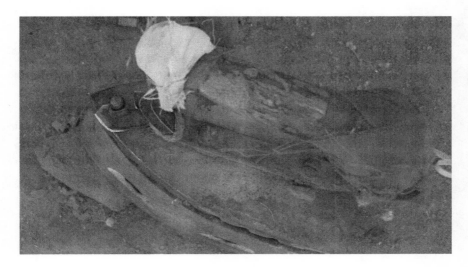

Bernie stopped at a coke stop and while sipping on his drink, he noticed an elderly man sewing on a very primitive sewing machine; he sat down to visit him for a while. If you're thinking that the sewing machine might have been a museum article, take a look at the iron he was using. A local guy came over and opened the top of the iron to light his cigarette from the hot coals – yes, the charcoal provided the heat – imagine this is still in use. Bernie thought about purchasing it, but then again, where would the old man buy another one?

While Bernie was visiting with this older man, a young boy about three years old came up to Bernie and was fascinated with Bernie's tattoo, a picture of a bike on his left calf. The young child started touching the tattoo as if it belonged to him. He would cover it with his two small hands hiding it from the other kids who had gathered around. It became his toy for a few minutes.

While talking about irons – since our tour began in Cairo, we have not had our clothes washed or dried in machines – all by hand. We have it done by the locals whenever possible, and lately it has been coming back wet. If the sun is not shining when they hang the clothes out to dry, it is our problem, not theirs. You see clothes hanging on trees, fences or just lying around on the grassy areas. Lately, because we are in the rainy season in Tanzania, everything is damp; tent, sleeping bags, mattresses, clothing, and they all stink. You can bet our clothes never saw an iron all across the continent.

When cycling solo most of the time through Tanzania, we have lots of time to think about all sorts of things and Bernie mentioned that he passed an elder Masai who smiled and showed that he had only 'one' tooth. Many younger people have stained teeth and I'm rather certain that they do not brush their teeth. However, had this elder used a toothbrush, it would have been the correct terminology. Because, really, when we have all our teeth, we should be calling it a teethbrush. You can see that we sometimes didn't do too much deep thinking – maybe that is why we were enjoying this adventure. Like I said, we felt like we were twelve years old with Tour d'Afrique as our parents – waking us up in the morning, preparing our meals, and telling us where and how far to go.

Malawi — Tea Plantations

Fertile Land!

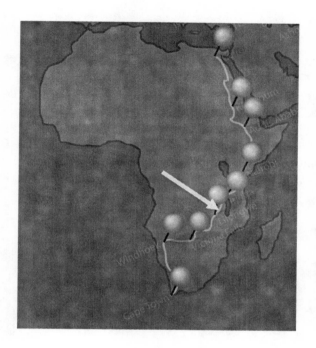

Enter: March 27, 2008 Exit: April 4, 2008	
Rough Roads (clay/washboard/sandy – (km)	0
Pavement – (km)	771
Total Distance – (km)	771
Number of Cycling Days	6
Population – millions	13

UPON ENTERING THE COUNTRY OF MALAWI, WE WERE PLEASED TO LEARN THAT we would be staying at a beach resort for two nights, which would give us a rest day enjoying the beach. The road from the highway to the resort was a bit of a surprise, it was just over a kilometer in deep sand. Cycling was virtually impossible, but hey, a nice walk while Bernie was dreaming of a cold beer; it was worth it. On this rest day, the tour operators organized a beach party, with loud rockin' music.

The Malawi countryside is very lush, with many tea plantations, where we see workers in the fields with baskets strapped to their backs. This densely populated land-locked country is heavily dependent on agriculture with around 85% of the population living in rural areas, their most important crops being tobacco, tea, and sugar. It is very evident the country has a reforestation program in progress — there has been much clear-cutting, replaced by young trees growing all at the same height.

For a number of years, Malawi has depended greatly on international aid, and still does. We learned at a pre-dinner information session, given by one of our support staff, that in 2006, the government decided to provide virtually all farmers with fertilizer (not just the larger or more successful ones). It goes without saying that the fertilizer was, of course, used to re-energize the land and boost crop production. This new strategy was undertaken to hopefully avoid having to provide food aid when crops failed or were too meager to support the people. It worked very well, in that, not only are the grain bins full, but also Malawi has become a net exporter of food to nearby countries. I suppose the lesson learned is that, if you give people the opportunity to become more self-sufficient and less dependent on aid, most often they will be more productive and take greater pride in themselves.

I guess my parasite was getting the best of me; I had not been feeling well (stomach sickness) for the past week with no sign of getting better — no appetite and therefore too weak to cycle the hills of Malawi. We left the beach resort on the truck and were pleased to find a hotel room at our next campsite in Mzuzu, which was part of a hotel complex. Arriving at camp early, we booked into a room and I went straight to bed, not to get up again until the next morning, with my best buddy, Bernie, looking after me. He left with our plates to pick up our dinner from the truck. I told him that I would try to eat a bit, so he planned to eat with me in the hotel room and was looking forward to sitting on a real chair at a table. He returned to the room with our plates loaded with food and as soon as I smelled it, I got sick. He had to leave the room quickly, disappointed, he went to the bar, ordered a beer and ate the two plates of food himself as it was a 'no-no' when it came to wasting food.

The next morning, we decided to leave the tour for the next three days taking an 11 hour bus ride from Mzuzu to the capital city of Lilongue, thus giving me a rest from cycling – surely, my health would improve as I was still struggling with my food intake and keeping it down. The bus ride provided us with another adventure we would not have experienced had we cycled – we made the best of everything. When we arrived at the bus station, we were swarmed by a number of bus drivers and their helpers wanting us to choose their bus. They didn't even know where we were going; they just wanted our business. Once seated on the bus that was headed to Lilongue, we waited for about two hours to depart, as there was no exact departure time, just when the bus was full. While we waited in the bus, we were entertained with all the vendors walking along the sides hoping to sell us water, juice, bananas, mangos, coke, and fanta. I noticed one lad who had three large open egg crates, filled with eggs, and I thought; who would purchase eggs while riding on a bus? They don't give you the carton with the eggs, just hand them to you in a paper bag, sure to get broken when they jar each other. My question was answered later as we were riding through the countryside; the person across the aisle from me had purchased some eggs and they turned out to be hard-boiled. Before eating them, she sprinkled some salt over them from the small bag of salt that came with them – a healthy snack, don't you think?

The bus made many stops along the way, mostly picking up people, all headed for the big city. We were amazed, asking ourselves, where are they going to put these new passengers? When we reached Lilongue, the aisle was full of people sitting or standing – no space wasted. A woman was sitting on her luggage in the aisle next to Bernie and was passing her time knitting. Bernie began talking with her asking where she was going, where she lived, how many children she had, the usual stuff. He then asked her if she would teach him how to knit. She showed him a few stitches, knit one, purl two. After passing her knitting back to her, he turned to me and said, "Who knows, I may take up knitting and one day knit you a dress, and I hope it's a size 10 or smaller."

Bernie had a bottle of Malawi Gin, and at a couple of road stops, he was able to purchase a cold lemonade-type soft drink. Ah, a gin and tonic – almost tonic – life was good, at least for Bernie. We also made a few bathroom stops; alas, sans salle de bain, just the roadside and if lucky, a bush for the gals to seek some privacy.

When we arrived in Lilongue, we found a very comfortable hotel with beautiful bed linens, of which I made good use. The sign outside the hotel indicated that there was TV service; we were looking forward to catching up on a bit of news. However, there was no television reception and we therefore phoned the front desk. We were told that the television had not worked for the past year, as they had had an electrical storm in 2007 and had not gotten around to repairing the service. They made it clear that it was not their fault that the town experienced an electrical storm, again, our problem, not theirs.

We were able to get accommodation for one night only at this nice hotel with great linens, so we decided to join the tour at their hotel/campground facilities where we were able to rent a room and would you believe, they had WiFi service – it was great. Over the course of our two nights and one day at the hotel, my health improved, allowing us to use our room as an internet café. I had my computer hooked up full time to the internet and the riders had full access to our room to drop by and get in touch with their friends and families.

Many of the cyclists visited the downtown core of the Capital City of Lilongue and mentioned a wonderful Italian restaurant – a must. My long rest was proving to be just what I needed, and I actually felt hungry, so we decided to take them up on their recommendation. When we arrived, I felt great, was actually hungry, and knew that I should eat. Bernie ordered a pepper steak and I got the most expensive item on the menu – prawns in lemon sauce and a glass of white wine. Before the meal arrived, I nibbled on a piece of bread; it tasted doughy, and my nausea returned. I just could not eat another morsel, so Bernie ended up eating two meals again and drinking the wine. In a sick way, I think he was enjoying the fact that I had a tender stomach. The next day, Bernie went downtown with a cycling buddy of his and bought me a get-well card and a beautiful painting of three zebras – a nice touch and a great pick-me-up.

Bernie's 'nice touch' proved to be just what I needed. The next day I was back on my bike looking forward to some half days, just taking my good ole time riding along enjoying the countryside, small villages, meeting the rural people. While riding along, it occurred to me that we had not seen a driveway since leaving Cairo. Then again, no one has a need for one, as there are no vehicles in the small villages we passed through – just big trucks. Obviously, their owners were not from these small villages. We have not seen a baby-stroller as babies are carried on the backs of women and children. You will never see male adults carrying a baby on their backs, and rarely anything on their heads – it seemed that task is left for the women and children.

While taking a short rest on the road one afternoon enjoying an energy bar, Bernie and I were joined by five young girls. Bernie asked them if he could take their picture and, of course, they all laughed and were excited when they saw themselves on the screen. While Bernie was giving them each a coin worth about 10 cents, each girl put her hand out and when given the coin, closed her hand and curtsied to us. You will notice in the picture, opposite, that their hands are closed with a coin in each. We could be giving money to children at every turn – on this occasion, these girls were alone with no other children in sight. We would have been mobbed, otherwise.

Further on, we stopped and talked to some kids on their way to school; all wearing uniforms, usually blue pants and skirts and white shirts. One kid had his lunch with him – it was a shucked cob of corn tied to a string around his neck, ready for a quick snack — no fast foods at their school cafeteria. We still kick ourselves for not getting a picture of this unique snack. A little further along the road, a teenage girl came out of her house, and did a little dance for us – just having fun, but hoping for some coins to be thrown her way.

We were met by young men transporting large amounts of water on bicycles. Bernie estimated that they had about 35 to 40 gallons of water mounted on a rear rack on their bike. A jug hung on each side of the tire with about 10 gallons of water in each, and on the top a huge plastic 20-gallon pail – so they had about 400 lbs. mounted on these steel-framed

Chinese-made bikes. While riding downhill at very fast speeds trying to keep the bikes from fishtailing, you could hear the hum of their tires from quite a distance.

The use of the plastic 'gerrycans' has had, in reality, a profound affect on the way water is obtained. In the 'pre-gerrycan' years, women had large earthen jugs, some of which are still being used. These jugs are too heavy for children to carry, so the women were the principal water fetchers. Plastic jugs are now available everywhere, allowing even small children to fetch water. Although this helps the women with this chore, unfortunately, it often takes these kids away from their school attendance.

Throughout most countries we have cycled, we would occasionally meet three or four women walking together. The ages of these women sometimes seemed to be about 10 years apart from each other. Bernie speculated that they were probably the wives of one individual. He would often throw a kiss at the older women and there would be much laughter among the women, no doubt cajoling the older women that she *still had it*.

The children are very creative when it comes to making their own toys. We have met a number of them pushing homemade scooters and little cars made from twigs with plastic bottle caps for the wheels – no store-bought toys in this neighbourhood. We take their pictures and, of course, give the boys some money for allowing us. You still see children playing hopscotch, skipping ropes, pushing bicycle rims with a stick, and playing with buttons on strings, again, much like the 50s on Prince Edward Island. On the tour so far, we haven't seen too many people wearing sunglasses or smoking cigarettes, nor have we seen a lot of obesity. Notice the boys' western style clothing.

One afternoon we met up with a man who had a team of oxen pulling a cart loaded with long pieces of lumber. At that very moment, one of our tour vehicles pulled up behind us. I believe the owner of the team was switching the oxen from one side of the road to the other and upon seeing the truck, the oxen spooked, ran up a dike and the cart swung around and the lumber hit the side of our truck. We watched while the driver stopped and checked the damage – a few scrapes. No exchange of insurance information done in this country – our driver just drove on.

That same day, we found ourselves in a small town and decided to stop at one of their roadside cafés – felt like we were on a 'real vacation', taking the time to sit at one of the outdoor tables to enjoy a coke. We were used to locals coming up to us selling their wares. This one young lad approached us with a homemade soccer ball for sale – he was obviously a bit high on something, but he spoke very good English. Bernie's advice to him was that if he wanted to be a successful salesman, he must be more presentable and should start by zipping up his fly, as it was wide open. He zipped up and laughed – no sale to Bernie.

During one of our evening rider meetings, we were told by the tour leader that we were camping in an area that had a fair number of ticks and that we should check ourselves before getting into our sleeping bags to make sure we weren't carrying any on our bodies. Of course, we were diligent in doing so, checking sometimes two or three times before retiring. I was all tucked in, felt a tickle on my leg, and checked it out – yes, indeed, I had found one. You might imagine that I had a hard time getting to sleep that night. Of course, I was 'bugging' Bernie to ensure that he was free of the bugs. The next morning, no one complained about being bitten.

A gardening tip while on this leg of our trip; while cycling, we met many transport trucks, but one in particular had the dash covered with green peppers and tomatoes; a little hot house on the move. We thought that my brother, back on PEI, could put his dashboards on his fleet of vehicles to better use. Many of the tour buses and trucks, called lorries in Africa, are laden with religious articles – many look like shrines.

Quite often on this tour, I think of my Mom and Dad. On this tour, every morning we usually have a large pot of porridge staring at us as early as 6:30 a.m. That's when I think of Dad – back in the late 50s and early 60s, when I had to make breakfast – and quite often the porridge was not up to his standards; too lumpy, forgot the salt, or just not cooked enough – Dad was not a happy camper when this happened. I think of Mom more often at lunchtimes when we stop at the roadside lunch truck and almost daily they have sliced cucumbers and I make myself a sandwich – Mom loved cucumber sandwiches.

ZAMBIA — VICTORIA FALLS

Cycling the Hol(e)y Roads

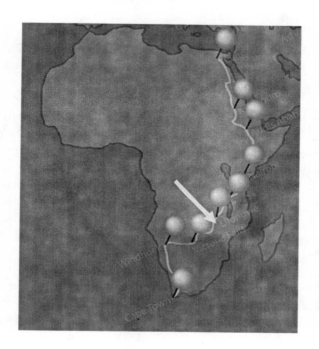

Entry: April 4, 2008 Exit: April 15, 2008	
Rough Roads (clay/washboard/sandy – (km)	0
Pavement – (km)	1,154
Total Distance – (km)	1,154
Number of Cycling Days	8
Population – millions	12

Entering Zambia, we took advantage of the working pace of the immigration officers. While waiting for our visas to be issued, Bernie spent his last few Malawi Kwachas buying beer for some of the Tour d'Afrique work crew – after all, we have to ensure that we stay on their good side. Lately, we've been staying at some nicer campgrounds, but with "nicer" comes more expensive beer – the $0.90 beer suddenly became a $2.50 beer; thank God I haven't acquired a taste for it yet. We have five days of cycling to our next rest day near the capital city of Lusaka. From Lusaka, we will be moving on to Livingstone for a two-day rest to visit Victoria Falls, another Natural Wonder of the World.

When entering a border crossing, you can imagine some of those entry points were not very busy; as the tour's route found us mostly 'off road' in very rural areas. As soon as we exited one country and entered another, the moneychangers swarmed us. Unlike the developed world, where we use banks to exchange our currency, most often, there are no banks in the small border towns and the local moneychangers are waiting for you. You have to be very astute when converting currency and calculating the exchange rates. In our case, Bernie took this job on all across the continent – he made the purchases and did the bartering. When approached by one of these moneychangers, you had to be quick, because they increased the exchange rate from one person to another, depending on your body language and facial expression. A 'rule of thumb' was when you did agree on a rate, you never gave them your money before you had their money in your hand. They would sometimes make an excuse to leave and obtain more local currency, or some similar excuse, and then they were gone, never to return. We did have an incident at the Zambian border where the police were called in, the money thief was caught, and the rider given the correct amount owed to him.

The countryside of the last three countries (Tanzania, Malawi, and Zambia) had many similarities – I found that Tanzania is the prettiest and more cultivated while Malawi has a better lumber and reforestation plan, rather than the 'slash and burn' method used decades ago. In Zambia, one of the poorest countries in Africa, we noticed that the charcoal business was certainly alive and thriving. Besides subsistence farming, the Zambians were busy in the wooded areas cutting branches from the trees, transporting them to their homes on their backs or heads, and charring them down to a lump of charcoal they use in their outdoor fireboxes. The thinly curved tree branches were ideal for turning into charcoal, their main source of fuel for cooking in the small villages and towns – we often saw bags of charcoal along the roadside for sale.

Of course, some trees had very straight branches, and were used as the basic structure for building their homes; no need for milling. The mortar between the studs was dried clay. Most homes in these southern countries have roofs made of corrugated steel, as well as the many thatched roofs we had seen along our route since leaving Cairo. As you've heard me say a number of times, the majority of these towns have no electricity or running water.

The next five days were extra long cycling days, the longest day being 195km – Bernie completed it in 8 hours and 52 minutes cycling time, plus time for a lunch break. The temperature averaged about 34°, with a high of 39°Celsius. When Bernie came into camp that aftern oon, he was wiped. I had to get him his soup and dinner and he was in bed snoring by 7:30 p.m. I was able to do the chores that evening, as I had just cycled the first half of that long day, about 110km. The next day, I joined him and we rode 85km. The following day out, after about 50km, my chain broke (just too much power in my legs, I guess). We might have been in trouble; we had broken our chain-link repair tool way back in Addis Ababa, but fortunately, fellow cyclist, Bruno, was right behind us (by the way Bruno has everything, even a broom and dustpan for his tent). He and Bernie fixed the chain in a few minutes and all it cost was a hug from me and a beer from Bernie later when we got back to camp.

With just a little over four weeks left on the tour, our minds are slowly reverting to the western world. We are now in Lusaka, the capital of Zambia, the most western-like city since we touched down in Frankfurt, Germany, on our way to Cairo back in January. We have not seen a parking lot since then, and today we visited a western style mall with a huge parking lot – wow – the things you take for granted. Another 'first' today was seeing a lawn mower, but then again, there is no need to have one in Egypt, Sudan, or Ethiopia. We also noticed that in Lusaka, life must be more prosperous, because we immediately noticed that some of the woman were a little on the heavy side – something we had not seen on our path through the previous countries. We noticed a gradual increase of goods and products available to us as we continued to move south, a reminder of all the comforts we have missed since leaving Cairo.

We just got back from that western-style mall. We each enjoyed a latte; Bernie had a banana split and I had a fruit cup with ice cream. Some of you will say "big deal!", but we haven't had many treats like this since leaving Canada. The thought just occurred to me that we were sitting enjoying our coffee and ice cream and just 100km outside of Lusaka, where we had just cycled, the people had *nothing* – were just living off the land. Their homes are built totally from what nature provides them, living very harmoniously with nature. The only thing they have that does not come from the land is their clothes, and they are mostly used western clothing. This is where you see the children wearing sports t-shirts from North American soccer and hockey clubs. A sharp contrast from the city.

I haven't talked very much about the wonderful group of people with whom we lived with during this winter of 2008. Our number has increased to just over 70 riders, along with support staff of about 15. We expect another dozen to join us before we reach Cape Town. Among the riders, we have many professionals – a lawyer, engineer, dentist, doctor, university professor, investment consultant, accountants, students, and some retirees, like us. The majority of the group is young (ages 22 to 45) – all gung-ho – they can party late into the night and ride all the next day – we love them. We, on the other hand, might occasionally stay up until 8:30 p.m. – that is late for us!

Since the start of our tour, I have had one flat, Bernie, seven (all on rocky roads). Bernie has had two falls, both in sand, and nothing serious. I've had about six falls – only one serious, while cycling in Ethiopia, requiring ten stitches. I am not the only one who had to have stitches — our top racer took a nasty spill in Ethiopia while avoiding a goat, and required stitches as well. There were many falls among the riders – one person got a bad infection as the result of a fall and had to go on IV and antibiotics for a few days; she was lucky she got treatment for the infection early on. One of the riders dislocated his collarbone (he fell when his bike didn't negotiate a speed bump), and he had to take a few weeks off. Another cyclist, while avoiding a child on the road, found himself about to be run over by a 4x4 and, of course, wiped out; fortunately, the truck missed him; his helmet took the brunt of the fall, and that is what saved him. Oh yes, helmets, the tour operators were very diligent that no one, absolutely no one, was allowed to ride without a helmet; if they insisted, they would have had to leave the tour. There were also lots of road rash incidents and a fair number of people with infected mosquito bites – malaria pills, what a blessing. We're getting to know our limits – just what exactly we can and can't do. As I have been saying, we sometimes cycle the morning or afternoon only – and when we're feeling well, of course we stay on our bikes the whole day. There is always the pressure not to jump on one of the trucks, but we are beyond that pressure.

I mention road rash, I do have *the* road-rash story of the tour to tell you. I got permission from the individual, who was the brunt of it, to tell you his story. I take you back to Sudan when we were on very flat, almost new pavement that had just been laid by the Chinese, who are building some road infrastructure in that country. The tour operators had warned us about 'drafting' vehicles – the rule was *'don't do it'*. We were also warned about holding onto vehicles (or cattle) while cycling uphill – another no-no. Well this one day, this individual found the opportunity impossible to pass up, and found himself behind a big truck that was moving along at a good pace. Here is the story 'in his words'.

Fighting a strong headwind on a flat road approximately 140km southeast of Khartoum, a boring, tedious ride, was made (briefly) much more fun by the thrill of tailing an 18-wheel tractor-trailer at a range of about 4 feet and at a speed of roughly 60km per hour. This was my first and LAST experience with drafting in Africa. It was about six minutes of pure road-racing ecstasy....followed by a slide that seemed to last about as long. My front tire had a sudden encounter with a muffler that suddenly appeared in my path from under the truck. I actually didn't go back to inspect the "killer muffler" as it was too far away to bother by the time I stopped sliding. Let's not forget that aside from bodily injuries, my right bar-end was removed and right handlebar was 1/4 inch shorter. My derailor was shorn down so as to be almost useless and my back shifter-cable was shorn right off and needed replacing. My front rim was CRACKED (not just dented) and I lost four spokes, yet somehow my tire was still inflated and I was able to ride the remaining 3km (slowly) to the lunch truck. Luke, our bike mechanic, was first on the scene, attempting to administer medical treatment prior to Doctor Luke (yes, same name as bike mechanic, Luke) and our nurse, Amadine, took over. My three least favorite moments after the slide that lasted an eternity were: 1) puking while the wounds were being cleaned, 2) cutting my hand open while trying to change the battery in my flashlight that same night, and 3) changing the dressing two days later in the shower at an Ethiopian brothel in Metema - yuck.

We left the city of Lusaka, and its cappuccinos and ice cream, without incident. There was no need for a police convoy, as our exit route was straightforward. One of the tour operators remained in town to do some last-minute errands. He was driving a smaller support vehicle, dubbed the *Bushbaby*. While leaving the city, his left rear tire fell off and rolled into a pedestrian, knocking the pedestrian down and injuring him. The accident immediately drew a crowd of spectators, something like what had happened to me back in Ethiopia. The driver quickly left the vehicle to check on the pedestrian's condition. In the meantime, a couple of men jumped into the truck and stole whatever they could get their hands on: cameras, a blackberry, two phones, the driver's passport, and a substantial amount of money. They even went so far as to rob the injured man who was lying on the ground. The police came on the scene and took our tour operator to the police station for questioning. He managed to get his passport back, but nothing else.

When we were cycling through Zambia, we encountered a roadblock set up by local authorities, where all the cyclists were held in an area for about two hours. We were asked to produce our passports and our $50. receipt for our entry visa, when clearing immigration. We were told that our delay was caused by a mathematical error at the border; the charges for the number of visas didn't match the number of cyclists. We knew it was certainly an internal problem; however, we still had to play by the rules. The stop was not too taxing, although it was very hot and meant a late entry into camp that evening.

We were always a great curiosity for the locals when we stopped at the road stops along the way. The people would just stand around, some staring at us, not speaking until spoken to, especially the children who were very shy. I suppose we looked a bit strange to them though – they rarely saw any tourists passing through their small villages. This one time, while I was sitting and drinking my coke, I watched a young woman directly across the street piling big truck tires on top of each other. She managed to pile four tires high, just above her waistline. I wondered what she was doing – certainly not setting up a cooking area – not on tires. She then laid a huge bowl-like pan on the tires and filled it with water, setting up a washing stand for her daily wash. It appeared the tires were a shared commodity – a portable table (adjustable, depending on your height) easily rolled from hut to hut. Another example of making most of what you have.

The road leading into the touristy town of Livingston was absolutely terrible – we nicknamed it the *Hol(e)y Road* – there were so many potholes. We came upon three local boys (age 15 or 16) digging earth from the sides of the roads and dropping it into the holes as we approached them. Their hands would then be extended asking for money for their efforts in making our trip a little easier. It seemed like that was the government's way of repairing the roads – there was no sign of maintenance crews anywhere. Bernie loved dodging the potholes – he compares it to a WII computer game – hmmm, could be a possibility.

The Hol(e)y Roads led us to the Livingston Safari Lodge and campgrounds, near Victoria Falls, where we stayed for two days. We were fortunate to be able to get a private lodge with a zebra theme – very African – a large room with a 20-foot ceiling, two double beds complete with mosquito netting — a nice bath, shower, flush toilets, and *hot water* on demand, with internet to boot.

We made good use of our first rest day and signed up for a 'wine and cheese' trip down the Zambezi River – about 20 fellow cyclists on four rafts. We hoped to see some wild animals and different species of birds; we had been told that the crocodiles did not like lifejackets and were not fussy about drunken people – at least that's what the locals said.

There were six of us on our raft, and we managed to pass around wine and cheese while drifting down the river skirting small rapids – it was great fun, lots of laughs. We saw hippos, crocs, and elephants on the riverbanks. After drifting/paddling about 12km down to the Falls, we came ashore some distance before the edge of the Falls, listening to their roar. We were told that elephants often cross the river between Zambia and Zimbabwe, and every now and then, some go too close to the Falls and are swept over to their obvious death.

Our guide, who spoke very good English, entertained us with stories as he guided us along the river. Apparently, a number of years ago, in one of the parks, all the elephants had been poached off. Later, the government decided to restock the park; however, they did so with young bull elephants, forcing them to leave their herd at an early age, making it easier to capture and relocate them to the park. These young bull elephants had no mature elephants to discipline them, in particular, a matriarch. Some of them started mating with female rhinos and because of the elephants' much heavier weight, were fatally injuring the rhinos. The park officials then decided to bring in a mature herd of elephants and the young bulls were disciplined and I suppose told by the matriarch that elephants don't fornicate with rhinos, and it worked – our guide assured us that this was a true tale.

After a very full breakfast at our lodge on our second rest day, we headed out to Victoria Falls and spent a couple of hours walking along the pathways and stopping at the scenic outlooks, being soaked by the mist and what sometimes felt like buckets of water pounding on us. We stopped at a very expensive resort at the Falls and had our always-favourite cappuccino and espresso in their lovely dining room. From the Falls, we stood on the bridge that connects Zambia with Zimbabwe and watched the bungee jumpers. We had about eight or so jumpers from our tour who were daring enough to take the plunge – young folk again – they have all the fun. The older folk stick to the wine and cheese on a raft.

While our young guys were jumping off the bridge, Bernie was creating a sideshow of his own. Young men selling copper bracelets constantly barraged us, all trying to outbid each other, each claiming that theirs were the best. They knew that Bernie was interested in purchasing a few, because he was asking them, "How much do you want for a dozen?" When the vendors heard that, they all rushed to him, arguing with each other, all saying, "I was here first." "This is *my* customer." and "My bracelets are the best." I thought we might have an outright fight — Zimbabweans against Zambians. We purchased about 36 bracelets from various vendors; the asking price was around $3, we usually paid about $1.50. One vendor would just not let us go, following us across the bridge back to our taxi. To get rid of him, Bernie said, "OK, I will give you $10 for 9 bracelets". The vendor replied, "OK". The deal was done and we were off. We must have bartered with these young men for about a half hour, again, a lot of fun.

While cycling in the beautiful countryside and through the Zambian towns, we saw many encouraging road signs. I share a few with you:

- Did you know that giving money, food and clothing to children on the streets, encourages them to remain on the streets,
- Fight Malaria, have your houses sprayed,
- Sex Thrills, AIDS Kills,
- Let us join in the fight against AIDS and Stigmatization,
- Vasectomies are for men who love their spouses,
- The problem of children on the streets is yours and mine; Don't be left out — Be Part of the Solution — Discourage: Begging, Alcohol and Drug Abuse, and
- I reject corruption, do you?

We have had ten more people join our tour in Livingston — mostly from France. Tomorrow, we cross the Botswana border and for the next five days, we will average 164km per day. Don't feel sorry for us — the countryside is flat and the prevailing winds are usually tailwinds — so it should be fun.

BOTSWANA — ELEPHANT HIGHWAY

Solitude on the Flat Roads!

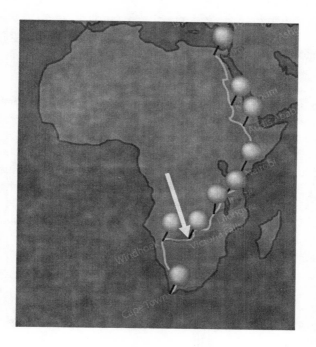

Entry: April 15, 2008 Exit: April 23, 2008	
Rough Roads (clay/washboard/sandy – (km)	0
Pavement – (km)	1,148
Total Distance – (km)	1,148
Number of Cycling Days	7
Population – millions	1.6

The last three countries on our tour (Botswana, Namibia, and South Africa) are much more developed than the northern African countries above the equator, giving us a greater sense of safety. Bernie and I have been cycling together (off and on) since the start; however, Bernie had become much stronger than I had, and therefore, his pace was faster. I had increased in strength as well, in spite of my stomach problems, but would never match him. He was constantly curbing his pace to keep me in his rear view mirror, and I found that I had to increase my pace so as not to make him stop so frequently. Therefore, the result was that we decided to cycle independently for the last three weeks.

> Feeling safer in Botswana, I will probably match up with other cyclists while Bernie struts his stuff keeping up with the crowd and completing full days on the bike. Because Bernie and I cycle single file and, therefore, don't chat along the route, we are basically cycling independently anyway, and because I have the support of the tour people, I feel very comfortable in letting him go ahead. My plan is to set out with him in the early morning, and he has agreed that he will move on when I start to slow down. I will just take my time, cycling to the lunch truck and possibly riding the lunch truck to camp, passing Bernie along the way. A number of other cyclists often accompanied me on the truck, and, of course, we joke around while riding through the countryside. I 'thought out loud' one day while sitting on the truck with these other 'truckers'. Seeing all my fellow cyclists peddling along on their bikes while I was sitting on the truck, I said it was a shame they hadn't purchased the *premium ticket* from Tour d'Afrique like I did – the 'premium ticket' would have allowed them to get on the truck, so they wouldn't have had to cycle every inch. That evening, while bantering at the campsite, some of the racers and EFlers didn't share my sense of humour with that one.

During these days where I saw my appetite and energy drop, especially at the half-day mark, I made more changes to my diet. Most evenings when lining up for dinner, I couldn't look at the food without getting sick. As we were travelling through countries that provided more amenities, I decided to purchase my own food and water. I just had to convince the truck drivers to allow me to stash it on the trucks wherever I found a few spare inches here and there (buying them the odd beer along the route paid off). I especially welcomed my newly purchased breakfast food, as I no longer could stomach the porridge. I even thought that our blue plastic dishes, which we had been using since day one, might also have been a factor, but I had to live with them until the last day. The combination of looking after my own food and drinking bottled water slowly brought me back to almost my old self.

Bernie has memories of Botswana and its elephants – we had wonderful times in the evenings sitting around the campsite; everyone was in great spirits knowing that we just had weeks to go before reaching Cape Town. Bernie wants to share this little piece with you.

We so looked forward to our first day in Botswana and opportunities to see wild elephants; the largest elephant population in the world is said to be in Botswana. Reportedly, there are 150,000 elephants in Northern Botswana, through which we were headed. The terrain was very flat, and having cycled through the mountains of Ethiopia, this terrain was rather boring. We peddled distances averaging 164km each day, so looking forward to seeing elephants lessened the boredom.

We saw no elephants the first day, but often did see piles of elephant poop. I imagined that if I had a pet elephant and walked it through the village of North Rustico; I would have to have Beryl follow me in the half-ton, as the run-of-the-mill pooper-scooper would not be the most efficient. Just as an aside, I read that in Sri Lanka, home to approximately 4,000 Asian elephants, a company has started a business recycling elephant poop into paper. Elephants, being true vegetarians, their waste are basically raw cellulose.

We stopped for refreshments at a service station and chatted with one of the locals, who told us we shouldn't camp in the open, because there were many lions in the area. We told him that the Tour decides where we camp and we have the utmost confidence in their decisions, our safety always came first.

When we arrived at camp, there was much talk of elephants and lions, but Beryl and I had to celebrate her personal best distance up to this point, 145km. It was hot, in the 30s, and Beryl's wine was well above room temperature. I still had some Malawi gin, but no tonic or mix of any sort except Gatorade crystals. After three attempts, I found the "perfect" formula; 1½ ounces of gin, two tablespoons of Gatorade crystals and three ounces of chlorinated

Botswana well water, all in my blue plastic mug, finger stirred and not shaken. I'm certain that with ice, it would have been awesome.

We pitched our tent very near the truck, and I quickly placed my sleeping bag closest to the truck in the event that, should a lion attack during the night, he could munch on Beryl and allow me time to cut my way out the side of the tent and scramble on top of the truck to safety; after all, I really wanted to finish the tour. Several of the less-brave cyclists slept on top of the trucks. During the night, bathroom duty for most of us was carried out not far from the tent, and I suspect that in some instances, just over the tent. I thought about having a pee inside the tent, using Beryl's water bottle, but in the near darkness, I couldn't be certain that it wasn't mine.

I will always have great memories of Botswana because of this one special time. On this particular day, while cycling on the flat pavement, not too hot with very little breeze – you might say perfect – I left the lunch truck cycling solo, setting Bernie free. My bike chain was rubbing constantly so I wasn't a popular person to cycle with for almost a five-day period. My bottom bracket was practically worn out and it wouldn't be replaced until we reached the City of Windhoek, the Capital of Namibia. While cycling along in pure solitude for about three hours, I was constantly dodging the thousands of corn beetles who were getting warmth from the pavement while cannibalizing the ones who had been crushed under the wheels of big trucks, oh, those pure buggers. I also was in the company of thousands of butterflies; disturbing them while cycling close to the roadside bushes where they were perched. There was so much of nature around me, in absolute silence.

Very few people passed me and I wasn't catching up to many people either, so there was a short period of time when I felt secluded and a little insecure. However, every now and then, a fellow cyclist would pass me, assuring me that I wasn't lost. It was mid-afternoon; I thought that I had had enough and decided to stop by the side of the road and wait for the last truck, which would be coming along within a half hour or so. I sat down beside a tree that had been knocked down, possibly by elephants. I spent the whole time corralling some of those corn beetles that are a mainstay on the Botswana highways. I built a small fence with twigs and corralled about 100 plus beetles. I mention this story, because I have never felt so at peace with myself as when doing this small and simple task – my whole focus was on those beetles – being *'in the now',* feeling like a child. Of course, once I saw the truck approach, I freed the beetles. I still think of this activity, most often just before falling asleep – it has a very calming effect on me – an experience you cannot buy.

Bernie and I left camp early one morning, gently cycling along the Elephant Highway, which we had been travelling for the past two days. Day 1 – (95km) no elephants; day 2 (144km) – no elephants. About 30km into our ride on day 3, we stopped for a refreshment break along the highway and I ate a handful of peanuts that I had in my bag. Immediately, my stomach got sick (that old parasite again). It wasn't fair for me to insist that Bernie stay with me, as I would be moving slowly from then on.

My plan was to just mosey along and eventually reach the lunch truck at the 75km mark, where I would hitch a ride to camp. I was probably at the

50km mark of the day, when lo and behold, a huge elephant crossed my path about a hundred meters in front of me. I dismounted, fumbled for my camera, and snapped this picture. At first, I thought the elephant would approach me, but instead it just slowly moved directly across to the left side of the road, totally ignoring me, followed by another, and yet another. I watched six elephants cross the road (young and old). During this time, a few cars came along, slowed down, and in doing so, spooked the seventh elephant; causing him to remain on the right-hand side of the road.

I did not want to take the chance of continuing to cycle and find myself between the family members, as the six elephants were waiting for the seventh to cross. The matriarch of the herd suddenly made a loud trumpeting noise while lifting her ears and trunk and started running – in a direction I thought was toward me. I hastily turned my bike around while keeping an eye on the herd and realized that she was simply disciplining one of the teenage elephants, who immediately ran off into the wooded area.

My only option was to stand there and watch them, ready to cycle back to meet up with other riders or hail down the next local vehicle. About 10 minutes later, a group of riders caught up to me, noticed the elephants, but did not stop. I jumped on my bike, joined the tail end of their peloton, and got through the elephant path without incident. I'll have to say this was a bit scary and I was glad I took pictures to be able to back-up my story at camp that evening. Not everyone would have believed me, although I'm certain Bernie would have.

Botswana exports a large amount of beef to Europe, and therefore, is very careful in not allowing diseases to enter the country. They have roadside "hoof and mouth" checkpoints throughout the country where you have to cycle through a chemical bath and clean your shoes on a mat. Our trucks carry all our equipment (in red boxes and our permanent bags). Of course, our casual shoes are stored in these boxes and bags. When the trucks passed through these checkpoints, they had to empty all the boxes and bags and remove all footwear to be disinfected on the chemical mat.

Throughout this book, I have mentioned the many coke stops at which we stopped to sit and rest, sometimes on the ground, sometimes on hewn logs, metal stools, tree trunks, plastic chairs, you name it. The roadstop/bar in this picture had to be *the best* – it even had a swimming pool where a few of the riders jumped in still wearing their riding clothes. The sun was beating down on this very hot day; their clothes would be dry within minutes after getting back on their bikes.

The bathroom at this rest stop was a treat; providing toilet paper and even a lock on the door. There was a basket near the sink filled with condoms; the country is trying to fight the spread of AIDS – a sign of progress. Incidentally, approximately one in six in Botswana has HIV, giving the country the second highest HIV infection rate in the world, after Swaziland.

The above picture shows a 50-plus year old bird's nest. The owners, small 'social weavers', weave individual rooms in the nest – not unlike a modern condominium. It is very strong, standing up to strong windstorms and all other types of weather. While stepping under the nest to take this picture, scores of small birds escaped within seconds. One of their main predators is snakes who can "wind" themselves in and around each "condo" looking for their prey.

We found ourselves heading out on our last day in Botswana, which just happened to be the longest day's ride of the tour – 207km. Bernie left the campsite ahead of me, determined to complete the whole day, I left later after packing our belongings on the truck. As I mentioned earlier, Bernie looked after our money while on the tour, but for some reason I had all our Botswana Pulas on my person, in fact in my sports bra. I guess while breaking down our tent that morning, the money fell out of my sports bra and I never noticed it was missing until mid-day, a sure sign that I had lost just too much weight. The lost money was the equivalent of $40, the odds were it would be found by someone who greatly appreciated it – we considered it a donation.

At one of our last refreshment stops in Botswana, I was met by Bruno, a fellow rider, who arrived at the stop before me (he was the guy who fixed my broken chain way back in Zambia). Bruno had been collecting soccer shirts of the National Soccer Teams from all the countries we had cycled, however, he didn't get a chance to purchase one while in the bigger towns in Botswana and we were almost at the border.

Bruno came out of the store saying that the girl at the cash was wearing a Botswana Soccer Team shirt and he would have traded his cycling jersey for her shirt, but didn't want to give up his most treasured cycling jersey. I told him maybe I could trade with her, as I didn't mind giving up my jersey.

He was very surprised that I would consider this. I entered the store with Bruno by my side and asked her to trade; she drove a hard bargain – she would trade, but also wanted some money, which Bruno agreed to. She and I went to the back room and switched jerseys. That particular day, I was not wearing a cycle jersey, rather a golf shirt. So, if you are ever travelling through Botswana and come across someone who's wearing a green golf shirt from Rustico Resort Golf and Country Club, you'll know that it was once my shirt. A few days later at camp one evening, Bruno presented me with one of his cycle jerseys from Quebec, Canada, in thanks for my trade.

On this last cycling day in Botswana, Bernie did register his personal best, 207km, eight hours in the saddle. His day didn't start off too well though, when he was leaving the campground just at sun-up, he hit the one pothole in the road and was separated from his bike – a few scrapes, nothing serious, except he broke his sunglasses – a good excuse to buy a new pair in Windhoek. I succeeded in peddling to the 145km mark.

Our last campsite in Botswana was at a travelers' lodge, complete with bar and western-style washroom facilities. We were all happy campers in this lodge and found ourselves in a few good conversations, teasing and cajoling, as we were pretty well one big family by this stage of the tour – we knew each other surprisingly well and with only a few weeks left on tour, everyone was in good spirits.

Since leaving Livingston, six days ago, Bernie has cycled every inch. Because I am writing this book after the fact, I can say that Bernie never did get on the truck again – he cycled straight through to Cape Town. Here describes some of his thoughts and feelings while cycling in the southern part of the continent.

Leaving Victoria Falls behind us, we have had some very long days; six, seven, and even eight hours in the saddle, with a half-hour stop at the lunch truck, makes for a long day. The terrain is very flat, not much tail wind, just as the tour operators promised us.

The principal difference between motoring and cycling is obvious, mechanical versus human power. In a car you are usually in an artificial, air-conditioned controlled environment and have little contact with the surroundings, in other words you are a 'passive observer'. On a bike, you feel the wind and are ever aware of its direction. You sense the change in the type of pavement and are forever watching for and dodging the treacherous potholes. You also feel the temperature changes when you climb a steep hill or when the sun comes out from behind a cloud and the temperature seems to rise by 10° Celsius immediately. Another difference between riding in a car and cycling are the smells: flowers, crops, cattle, and the ever-present manure.

There are very few fences and very often, cattle and donkeys are by the roadside but are rarely hit; they know the rules of the road. When you meet the people, you smile and look them in the eye and usually get a smile and a wave back, and often, with the children in particular, a high-five. They love to touch the white folk.

When you are driving in a vehicle and you see road kill, it goes by in a flash, but on a bike at 25km/hr, you see the wounds and often where birds have picked at the carcass. On one occasion, I saw fresh road kill, a dog, with the blood oozing from his wounds. Maybe this isn't so exciting, but one can't get too much closer to their surroundings than this.

NAMIBIA — DESERT LANDSCAPES

Roller Coaster Hills!

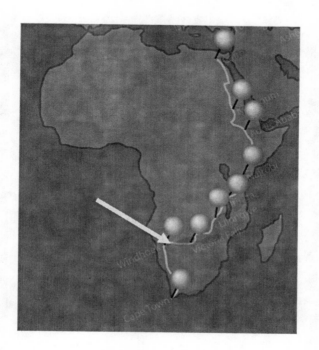

Entry: April 23, 2008 Exit: May 4, 2008	
Rough Roads (clay/washboard/sandy – (km)	295
Pavement – (km)	876
Total Distance – (km)	1,171
Number of Cycling Days	8
Population – millions	1.8

THE SURROUNDING NAMIBIAN COUNTRYSIDE REMINDED ME OF PARTS OF THE interior of British Columbia, Canada. After what seemed like more than 1,100km of flat roads in Botswana, it seemed like we were on a roller coaster as we passed through the canyons of Namibia. It felt like we were staring at the large hill in the picture above for about three hours before arriving at its base.

After leaving the beautiful graveled roads in the countryside and arriving closer to the capital city of Windhoek with a three or four kilometer descent into the city, we encountered speedy traffic and, being speedy, not too courteous to cyclists.

At the lunch break, about 70km from town, a middle-aged man, driving a half-ton truck, stopped at our rest stop and proceeded to give us a tongue-lashing for cycling on "his" roads. Shouting at us that we were a menace on the highway and some of us were sure to be killed. We listened to him rant on, but basically ignored him; he left in a fit of anger, peeling rubber. A few more cyclists arrived and told us about this same man coming up behind them and blowing his horn expecting them to get off the road. He was certainly an exception, though; most of the drivers would wait to pass us if there was oncoming traffic. There were, of course, a few exceptions;

Bernie was forced off the road a couple of times that day. Had he stayed on the road, he might have had a close call, but why take unnecessary chances. It always helps to have a rear view mirror to keep an eye on just how close the semis are behind you. All and all, though, we felt pretty safe on the highways. Many of the more experienced cyclists rode abreast of each other in a peloton; however, we were not that brave and made sure we cycled single file.

In Windhoek, we're staying at a very modern resort, with beautiful cottages (including satellite TV) and a campground. Since leaving Cairo, we have been living by the rule that on rest days, if one was sick, he/she would be on the top of the list for a room, as most of the hotels/resorts did not have enough rooms to accommodate everyone. Bernie and I, or should I say I, have made good use of this rule. This time, with both of us feeling OK, we opted to stay in our tent, thus freeing up a cottage for another fellow cyclist. The facilities provide us with all our needs; hot showers and flush toilets and even a laundry room with sinks so I can stand up to do the laundry chores, rather than squatting and pounding the clothes on a rock by a stream – stretching it there. There is a wonderful bar, with draft beer and a great restaurant with reasonably fast service.

Yesterday we took a taxi downtown to a very modern mall and walked around trying to find a bike shop or sports store. No luck with finding either, but we did bump into a vendor who was selling the identical napkin holders (animals carved out of wood) to the six that we had purchased while in Zanzibar - we needed two more. The vendor wanted $5 per carving and Bernie, who loves to barter, offered him $5 for the two; he came down to $7. Bernie told him that when he said $5, he meant $5, and then proceeded to place the napkin holders back on the table and start walking away. The vendor then shouted to him, "OK, because you're my first customer today, I'll let them go for $5." I figure that probably everyone is his first customer.

We took a cab to another beautiful mall, one of the best designed we have ever visited. We found a sports shop, bought some leg warmers, as it's very cool when leaving camp in the early morning, about 7° Celsius. One morning Bernie had to use his socks on his hands, because his full-fingered gloves were in the permanent bag on top of the truck. We took in our second movie in 2008; the movie wasn't great, but just sitting down in comfortable chairs for a couple of hours was a treat, and oh yes, popcorn.

We had an incident late one evening while at camp. Our cook, who slept on top of one of the trucks, arrived back in camp late in the evening and while climbing on top of the truck, fell and injured his head – had to have 10 stitches. Fortunately, he is OK, our biggest concern is, will he be able to properly feed us for the last two weeks, or will he forget the salt?

The first cycling day out of Windhoek, all riders reached camp before the trucks, carrying our equipment, arrived. They were late arriving due to a hold-up in Windhoek regarding proper licensing. We spent our time sitting and lying around resting while waiting for our camping equipment and food to arrive. A few of the racers decided to cycle on to the next campsite instead of waiting; by doing so, they clocked about 350 plus kilometers that day, booking themselves into a hotel. We met up with them the next day.

A couple of nights ago we had a wonderful evening. The tour operators rented a tour bus, which picked us up at our campsite (along with our cook and helpers) and drove us to the beautiful Fish River Canyon, second largest in the world and the largest in Africa, to have dinner while watching the sunset over the canyon – it was a fantastic evening. On the way back to the campsite, nature provided us with a spectacular thunder and lightning show.

At this point, I bring you back to Sudan. You recall when we were entering Sudan I thought Bernie was trying to get rid of me when he hid a bottle of scotch in my permanent bag, hoping that the immigration officers would find it and possibly shoot me. Well, that night, I was sure he hadn't given up and was still trying to do me in.

Upon arrival at our campsite from our excursion from the Fish River Canyon, we went straight into our sleeping bags – it was cold. Later on, through the night, there was a downpour and I got up to make sure the fly was secure on the tent, zipping all the door flaps and both air vents and crawled back into my sleeping bag falling asleep with the pelting sound of rain on the tent. A little later on, I woke up during the downpour and could hardly breathe, as Bernie had filled the tent with poisonous gas from his silent farts. In trying to get out as quickly as I could, I ripped the zipper on the inner door. I then opened the outer door flaps but couldn't repair the inner door zipper, so we were left open to the wilds. I didn't care if we got soaked and the armored beetles overtook our tent – I couldn't breathe. I was doing all this work in the dark and the rain – not taking the time to put my headlamp on. I looked over at Bernie, who was still sleeping – and noticed that he was wearing a gasmask — caught him in the act again. This story is 99% true.

We later found out that we had both ingested a parasite called Giardia lambli, better known as 'beaver fever'. It is a common cause of diarrhea and whose symptoms include the releasing of foul smelling flatus. This intestinal gas is produced by bacterial action on waste matter in the intestines and is primarily composed of hydrogen sulfide – a poisonous gas! Fortunately, for us, antibiotics took care of it.

One of our campsites in Namibia was at the railroad tracks in Gibeon. We had just completed a full day (175km), my personal best on the tour. Over the course of the last few weeks, Bernie had been composing a song while cycling solo in the beautiful countryside and it was planned that he sing his song sitting on the railroad tracks while our film crew captured him on tape. Arriving at the campsite late after this long day, Bernie immediately began to prepare himself for his performance; I believe this was downing two quick warm beers to ease the performance jitters. I got busy setting up our 'home' for the night. It was a grueling hot day but Bernie found the energy to give a good performance.

After the recording was completed, we sat around with various individuals chit chatting and toasting my personal best, and Bernie's performance. There were no facilities at this campsite and the ground was rock hard. Invariably, the "bathroom" topic came up. One of our fellow riders mentioned that he had already dug his hole in preparation for possible bathroom duty during the night. He mistakenly told me where he dug his hole – I told him that because of my grueling day, I did not have the energy to dig my own hole and planned to use his, so he had better dig another one – oh, life was so simple.

While cycling the dirt roads, the scenery was breathtaking. At first, it appeared as if you were cycling on the moon. We cycled through a few canyons where the hills on each side of us, rose up to 700 or 800 feet high. One afternoon, Bernie cycled about three hours, solo, no cyclists or vehicles – it was pure wilderness on the roller coaster hills. Because of this, he felt as though he had the planet all to himself, and like me, his thoughts fell back to his childhood.

It was the first day of school, September 1949. I was five years old and was very excited, however, not to start school. My four older brothers and two sisters were all at school and I was home alone with my Mom and had the pick of four bikes to test-ride. I can't recall which bike I borrowed, but it was probably Lou's because if he found out, my punishment would have been the least harsh, certainly a lot less painful than had I got caught "joyriding" with Aiden's bike. Unfortunately, neither of my sisters had bikes and the crossbar on a boy's bike presented me with a real challenge.

Our veranda was just the right height from the ground, so I leaned the bike against it and climbed onto the seat. My feet were a good distance from the pedals and with no handbrakes on those '49 models, my plan was to use the slight grade to the fence, coast up to and lean against it. Yes, it worked great! As my Mom was busy with her housework, I had several rides without her noticing me. I suppose I got bored with just going the 50 or so feet to the fence, so decided why not keep going through the gate, across the street and come to rest against the Cosy Corner Restaurant. Traffic was certainly not a problem, the tourists had gone, and there were only a handful of cars in the village anyway. I made it through the gate and across the street, but my speed was a tad faster than I had hoped and stopping at the restaurant was no longer an option. The creek next to the restaurant, and after which our village was nicknamed, the Crick, was my only option. Well, as I recall, the landing was soft, albeit somewhat wet, but I had twisted the handlebars and had to confess the adventure to my Mom, who straightened the handlebars while I cleaned off the muck. Man it was worth it!

Having just shared Bernie's story about his first bike ride with you, it may be a fitting place for him to tell you his story about how he purchased his first bike — somewhat fitting, as the memories came back to him while riding in the countryside seeing so many young lads with their bikes. Unlike Bernie's bike, though, which was used mostly for pleasure, their bikes were their only means of transportation and became their workhorse.

My first bicycle was a 1957 CCM men's, 'brand-spankin' new bike; purchased from the Woolworths store in Charlottetown, better known as the "five and ten" in those days. The cost, as I recall, was just over $50, which in 1957 was about two weeks' wages for a laborer. To earn this small fortune, I fished (jigged) cod with my Dad and Aubin Henry Douse. We'd leave Rustico Harbour at sun-up, around 5:30 a.m., and return about 12 hours later. Our usual catch was between two and three thousand pounds of cod, which was sold to Emmett Bob's factory for one and a half cents a pound. These were whole fish and, for hake, we received a cent a pound. We never fished on Sunday, and each Saturday we would try to get in before 5:00 p.m. to allow the factory crew to get home a bit early, clean up, and go out for a night on the town (that's another story). One Saturday, we were motoring back to the harbor and *about an hour from dock, we decided to try one last "bert(h)". Well we struck some bloaters, as we called the plus-20-pounders. We fished for over an hour and I landed my personal record, weighing in at 59 lbs. Because we were late landing our catch, a few of the factory crew had to work late, and I can still see the look of displeasure on Arliss's face; but I think he understood that, "Ya jist can't leave em when dare bitin' tight line".*

After I had amassed the huge sum of about $60, which was my summer's wage, it was time to make the trip to Charlottetown to purchase my bike. It was common knowledge that on every Wednesday afternoon, our local grocery store merchant, Alyre Gallant, made his weekly trip to the wholesale grocery in the capital city some 25 miles south of the 'Crick'. He agreed to give me and a friend, Joseph (Boy) Pineau, a lift to Charlottetown and transport both of us and the bike back to the village. That night my bicycle was resting against the same veranda from which I had taken my first solo bike ride eight years earlier. The next day at sun-up, I peddled from our driveway and coasted down the hill sporting a wide grin.

For my sixtieth birthday, I got a tattoo of a 1957 CCM bicycle on my left calf (as shown in earlier picture). When I first showed my tattoo at work, I was asked, "At your age, why did you get a tattoo?" I replied that as both my parents have passed on, they couldn't stop me. I also mentioned that the 1957 bike had road tires, which look great on my tattoo, but in 25 years or so, they'll probably look like knobbies.

It seems that I've always enjoyed cycling, and when I think back, my Dad often cycled in his younger years. I recall him telling us kids that when he first left home, he worked as a farm laborer and, not having a car, he would cycle to work a distance of twenty-five miles or so. In the thirties, his bike had one gear and the brakes were on the pedals, not unlike many of the bikes in Africa today. In the late 70's, Beryl and I and our two sons were visiting PEI on our holidays, and Dad, who was by then almost seventy and hadn't cycled for many years, asked me if he could try out my bicycle. He wanted to visit his nephew in Mayfield, a distance of about five kilometers containing a few hills. When he returned, I asked him what he thought of the new ten-speed bikes. He said he didn't use but one gear and as it had no brakes, he had to drag his feet going down the hill in order to make the turn onto the Line Road. I assured him that the bike did have brakes and then demonstrated the hand brakes mentioning that he was fortunate not to have experimented on the "hand mechanisms", especially the left-hand one (front wheel), while speeding past, what is now Pond Street.

Namibia has certainly been a treat – we cycled 850km in six days, 300 of which was over hard-packed clay roads, with sand, washboard, and lots of hills. Bernie is very comfortable cycling these roads and enjoyed them immensely – can't say the same for me. He cycled the full 850 – I covered 503. Bernie's last day was 178km, 128 of which was hard-packed clay and the last 50km on pavement, but with a constant head wind combined with a 15km climb. It was the longest day on his bike, at 8 hrs and 58 minutes of cycling. When he arrived at camp, to celebrate, he had a double gin and tonic, three beers, a coke, and a double dinner. Still hungry when he got up the next morning, he had a glass of orange juice, half an orange, and half a chocolate bar. He then went for breakfast, which included four fried eggs, two 8-inch sausages, two large helpings of fried mushrooms and onions, two buns and three cups of coffee. Immediately after breakfast, he had a Richard-Dee chocolate ice cream and an orange pop. He then had a nap, as we were on a rest day.

Our last rest day, where Bernie had the huge breakfast, was spent just outside the South African border on the Orange River, where we rented a thatched roof unit overlooking the River where they have adventure excursions. We declined signing up for the adventure; we saw a few people tip over in the cool water every now and then – didn't need that.

SOUTH AFRICA — OUR DESTINATION

Breezing along the Eastern Atlantic Coast!

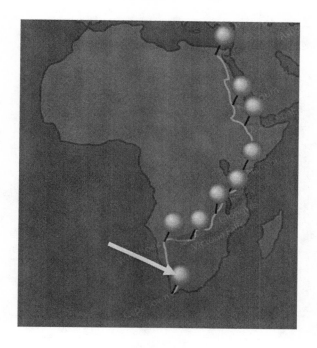

Entry: May 4, 2008 Arrive at Destination: May 10, 2008	
Rough Roads (clay/washboard/sandy – (km)	0
Pavement – (km)	745
Total Distance – (km)	745
Number of Cycling Days	6
Population – millions	44

LAUNDRY IS DONE, BIKES ARE TUNED, AND ALL IS READY FOR THE LAST six days of cycling on this fabulous journey. A 'must' before reaching Cape Town is picking up a pair of 'dress shoes' – and oh yes, a dress – to be ready for our farewell banquet upon arrival at the Waterfront. We girls were planning a 'grooming' evening the last night of camp – nail polish, the works. We wouldn't know each other! I hadn't had make-up on since arriving in Cairo back on January 9, and oh, where did I put my jewellery?

After three days of cycling in the scenic countryside, passing some of the beautiful South African vineyards, we found ourselves heading toward the Atlantic coast. Our first roadside stop was in the town of Vredendal at a well-known burger restaurant and convenience store called Wimpys. A pleasant surprise was meeting up with one of our truck drivers (nicknamed Wimpy) who had been with us for the first half of our tour (Egypt to Tanzania). Wimpy drove up from Cape Town to ride those final days with us. Of course, we kidded him that he had done very well, business-wise, owning these chain-store restaurants.

Much to our surprise, as we got ready to get back on the road, after our great cappuccino stop, the police arrived and advised us that we were not allowed to leave, as our Tour did not have permission to cycle on the roads in the Western Cape. Apparently, there had been complaints that many of the cyclists were cycling abreast, in peloton fashion, which they claimed posed a danger to all traffic.

While this was happening, the police also detained a half dozen or so of our cyclists who hadn't stopped at Wimpys. While waiting, these cyclists were invited to a tour and wine tasting by the owner of a nearby vineyard. Rats, we missed out on that, however, many of us enjoyed another breakfast and a cappuccino, not just the usual coke, sitting at Wimpys. It took almost two hours of negotiation by the tour operators before we were allowed to leave, in single file, with a police escort.

Although we didn't cycle through South Africa's leading wine area, some of our riders, after completing the tour, visited the vineyards in the Stellenbosch area just a short distance east of Cape Town, where many of the country's leading estates are located. We were told that the granite-based soils in the east are especially suited to the making of fine red wines, whereas the sandstone soils in the west are best for whites. God was very good to Bernie and me in that he allowed us to like both.

I have a story that has been on my mind while writing this book and I believe that now is the time to share it with you. This story has touched Bernie and me very much, and will always be on the top of our list as we continue to talk about these awesome four months of our lives.

Just over two months ago while sitting around our campsite in the hills of Ethiopia, we had the opportunity to chat at length with one of our fellow riders, Bent Nielsen. Bent, from Denmark, hails from an athletic background, where he has competed in many cycling competitions and has worked full-time for the Danish Cycle Federation as instructor for both children and adults. He has also been the organizer of several cycle races and triathlon competitions. Denmark and the surrounding countries are well known for their love of cycling and outdoor activities. It will not be a surprise to you when I say that Bent was among the racers on this tour, and was one of the few who were always vying for top spot.

Bent is very personable and told us that, since leaving Cairo, he had spent many hours on the road feeling very sad, even crying sometimes while cycling solo through the deserts of Sudan and the steep hills of Ethiopia. Bent missed his wife; this was the first major tour that he had undertaken without her by his side. He had lost her to cancer about a year ago and his wounds were still very close to the surface. She had been an athlete, like him, competing in many marathons, and they had shared a wonderful life together. I guess seeing Bernie and I enjoying ourselves together on our adventure further saddened him.

During the two weeks of our cycling hiatus, as we were not travelling through Kenya, everyone went their separate ways. Bent decided to go directly to Arusha, Tanzania, and set out to climb Mount Kilimanjaro, along with a few other riders, and from there he set up camp in the tour campsite for the remainder of the time to rest his legs. Bernie often said that Bent's legs looked like tree trunks, so powerful. During his stay in Arusha, Bent met a beautiful lady from the town, Whitness Simon Motica. They got to know each other over the short period of time, knowing that their time together would be brief as Bent had to continue on with the tour. When the tour departed from Arusha, they stayed in contact with each other via SMS and telephone. After two or three weeks, Bent missed Whitness so much that he invited her to fly down to Cape Town and meet with him at the end of our great expedition on May 10.

The reason I waited to tell you this story until now is that, about the fourth-last day of cycling in South Africa, Bernie and I were among the last few stragglers to arrive at the lunch truck. During lunch, we learned that Bent had still not reached the truck. This was very unlike him; he was usually one of the first riders to reach the lunch truck all the way across Africa. He finally arrived, hardly recognizable – he had stopped in at a barbershop for a shave and haircut, readying himself for his rendezvous with Whitness in Cape Town. No doubt, he was teased a bit. His plan was to arrive in Cape Town a day before the whole tour so he could meet Whitness at the airport. To do this, he had to cover a two-day distance in one day, which, of course, he did.

We said goodbye to Bent and Whitness in Cape Town and have since learned that they married and are living in Tanzania, with Whitness' son, Dishon. They have set up a safari business and are enjoying themselves immensely in Arusha. If you ever find yourself interested in climbing Mount Kilimanjaro, or a cycling adventure in Tanzania, check out their website, where they also have apartments for rent, at www.masaiapartments.com.

We thank Bent and Whitness for agreeing to share this story with you.

We've had a fantastic last week – a reason to celebrate everyday. Tour d'Afrique has certainly looked after us to the fullest – special meals and wonderful campsites along the Atlantic Ocean. It has been a bit cool, because the southern part of the continent is now experiencing their winter season – weather that we would get in October back in Canada – but I believe this is as cool as it gets for their whole winter. Why aren't we living here? I believe the Canadian winter of 2008 was "one to miss".

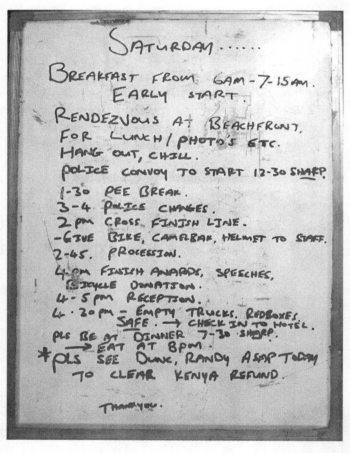

This was our last white board at our last riders' meeting, which we had every evening at camp for the past four months, outlining our next day's route. We knew we were going to miss those get-togethers that had become so much of a routine to us.

We made our last lunch stop about 25km outside of Cape Town on the Atlantic where we took many pictures on the beachfront.

Here are our three tour vehicles, and the smaller 'bushbaby' that accompanied us throughout the whole continent, carrying our gear, food, and water (and sometimes us).

A police convoy escorted us into Cape Town, and as usual, you will find me at the back of the convoy. We entered the waterfront to bands playing and boys waving flags from every country represented in the tour. This was followed by an awards ceremony for racers and EFI-ers (every "fabulous" inch), followed by champagne and hors d'oeurves. Everyone received a medal, even those who chose not to race or attain the EFI status. Total distance traveled – 10,385km (Bernie – 8,745: Beryl – 6,408). The media greeted us at the Waterfront, featuring the arrival of the full tour in the evening news.

We settled in our hotel, took all our personal belongings off the trucks, and prepared for our banquet dinner celebrating the end of the tour. We had met so many people and gotten to know some of them so well in the past four months. It was a bittersweet moment, to realize that the people we had lived with on this tour would all be going their separate ways; we had to believe that we would connect again with a number of them.

Our bikes were packed in cardboard boxes ready for the flight home, so we got back to doing what sane people do; we went to take in the markets downtown. Cape Town is a shoppers' delight – of course, some people who know me better and are reading this might ask, "Why is Beryl so delighted?

We purchased two wonderful pieces of art as mementos and gifts to ourselves, an eight-and-a-half foot giraffe carved out of kiaat (teak) wood, and a 50-pound hippo carved from ironwood. These carvings were shipped from Cape Town to Prince Edward Island – and both arrived intact. We have given them names: Gerome and Hilda, after two colourful characters that lived in our parents' generation on PEI – within sight of our retirement home on the Island.

We wondered what life would be like when we didn't have to breakdown our tent each morning, get on our bikes, and head off to a different location to set up our tent again. Cycling on a different route was often the motivation, which kept us going for the past four months forever looking for our daily 'finish' sign or the coloured ribbon directing us to our next campsite. A couple of things we will *not* miss; our blue plastic dishes and carrying toilet paper in every empty pocket – sometimes even stealing it.

It was sad leaving all those special people with whom we had spent the last four months; living closer than most families do. I am certain that when we meet these folks in years to come, we can pick- up on our relationship within moments, because we all shared an unbelievable time in our lives. We were careful not to leave our footprint throughout the whole continent, but we certainly left a part of ourselves in Africa. Incidentally, we each lost about 35-plus lbs. and each gained a parasite.

When we arrived at the airport in Cape Town, we unloaded our bags and bikes from the limousine and proceeded to our airline counter. As we were wheeling our belongings into the airport, two young local men met us and shouted "Bernie and Beryl, goodbye and have a safe trip." We looked at each other, puzzled – how did they know us? Then we looked at our bike boxes and saw that we had written on them in big bold black letters; Bernie and Beryl Doiron – Destination: North Rustico, Prince Edward Island, Canada.

REFLECTION

Back on the Red Soil on Prince Edward Island

OUR RETURN TRIP FROM CAPE TOWN WENT VERY SMOOTHLY – EACH leg of the journey was on time to the minute, and our luggage and bikes (all nine pieces) followed us as well. We arrived home to a wonderful reception, 'Welcome Home' signs at the airport and then again at our home in North Rustico.

We know that this adventure has changed us, but I can't put my finger on the change in me right now; maybe it's too early – need more time before I can describe how I feel. I certainly miss all the individuals with whom we spent four months. I have bouts of loneliness for the riders and the tour operators as we became very close with them. We also feel somewhat claustrophobic sleeping with walls around us each night.

Shortly after returning, we went for a cycle on our usual route on beautiful PEI – past golf courses, on to the rolling hills toward Stanley Bridge and then through beautiful Cavendish, home of Anne of Green Gables, followed by a gentle ride along the Gulf of St. Laurence before returning home. Throughout Africa, we never cycled the same road twice, except when Bernie got lost, and it felt strange to know every hill and turn that we would take on good ole familiar PEI.

In the coming weeks, we can sit back and reflect on the past four months and how this amazing trip has changed us. We were just talking this evening and mentioned that while we were on our bikes in Africa cycling through the country sides, in solitude with nature, you might say 'in the scene', it felt like we were in meditation – no one there to interrupt your thoughts – just living in the present and that is something we miss.

The above four paragraphs were written shortly after we returned from Africa, and I have not changed them. I am writing these words just over a year after returning to Canada, and I now realize why we were so happy on our fantastic adventure.

During the whole four months, we were one with nature, living outdoors 95% of the time, becoming less attached to material things. Perhaps that is why we saw so many smiles on the people as we passed through their small towns and villages; they were one with nature like the animals, birds, and insects – all living in harmony with mother earth. You may think I am going "off" a bit here; however, we didn't see many people living from one day to the next depending on pills, spending depressing hours alone in their homes. We could take a lesson from the African rural people on how to live with less – especially these days in our economic turndown. Seeing much of the continent from sitting on a bike cannot compare to other modes of travel, and the type of accommodations we had throughout the whole tour allowed us to gain a better appreciation of how the rural people in Africa still live today. The past four months felt like we were living in a time warp. In one's daily ordinary living, not much would happen in a four-month period, well these four months in our lives, were quite exceptional.

Can you imagine every evening for four months having dinner guests from every walk of life? Well, we did. The routine was, once you stood in line for your food with your camp stool tucked under your arm and picked up your food, you would look around and decide who you were going to dine with; as Bernie would sometimes shout "Who wants me?" Each evening brought new conversation as we continually learned more about each other. Sometimes the group numbered 75 or so, including tour operators. Being rather outgoing, Bernie and I thought this was such a treat, and we hadn't realized it until sometime later when we were back in the real world. If we were tired, or just plain bored with the conversation, we would just say "Good night," and go off to the tent to our favourite book. No one would ever feel that you were rude. Imagine doing that when you have dinner guests over to your home. Here everyone took leave whenever they felt like it; tired, bored, topic was of no interest or no reason at all.

I have talked a few times throughout the book about *living in the now*, and I believe cycling has taught me to calm my inner self, slowing down those racing thoughts that people experience in their everyday life. I will continue to cycle into my retirement years if only for that reason.

Bernie also had some reflection since returning from Africa. He share this with you.

> *One really appreciates the taken-for-granted amenities in our daily lives when they are unavailable for several days. For me, these primarily include a shower, flush toilet, and a chair with a back. But also, so many less essential items at our fingertips such as a cold drink or an ice cream cone. I'm not certain why there seems to be a great difference between not having something readily available and having something readily available and not using it. Why do we acquire so many items we rarely or never use? It must be our insecurity or maybe our hoarding instincts inherited from when our ancestors lived in trees.*

I want to share a poem that I think appropriately fits this book. My mother, Clarice Buote (Peters) (1920-2002) wrote this poem way back in 1974 and I'm sure would be proud to think that one of her poems was included in this book. Mom grew up on Prince Edward Island near the well-known Cavendish Beach area on the North Shore. What she says in this poem, about a time when she was a young girl, reminded me of the Ethiopian people, who walked long distances to their fields, to the water wells, and to their markets – day after day – we witnessed it as we cycled along.

A Day to Remember

This poem is about a day in my life that I'll always remember.
It happened in the Fall of '33 or '34 in the latter part of September.
My mother called me around five, to get up and have a bite.
My father was dressed and ready for our early hike.
I hurried and donned my overalls and potato gloves.
For it was kind of chilly. Just 24 above.

The basket wasn't very heavy when we started our walk.
But the farther we went, the heavier it got.
It was a sunny morning, the wind was rather brisk.
We were kind of tired when we reached Cavendish.
When we got there, we felt like we could use a cup of tea.
But to them we looked as healthy, as we could be.

We got to the field at seven o'clock; the drills were covered with frost.
The horse pranced around that old plough; he looked a little cross.
He took one look at that drill, the boss said "get'y up now".
His ears fell back, his nostrils flared, and you should have seen that plough.

We had to get down on our knees, to pull those sods apart.
We filled our baskets to the top, and dumped them in the cart.
The potatoes were so cold, our hands were so numb.
Before nine o'clock our fingers were all thumbs.
My kidneys always bothered me when I got cold feet.
So a high ditch, or a few trees was really a treat.

At ten o'clock they brought a lunch of sandwiches and tea.
This suited me well. By now I was starved you see.
This gave us a chance to stretch our legs and get the kinks out of our bones.
I was scared arthritis would set in before I reached home.
Only two more hours now till dinner, Oh, what a thrill.
Another cart load is gone. We start another drill.

I'd daydream a lot about what I would buy with my pay.
We had to be satisfied with a dollar a day.
I never lagged behind, always kept up with the rest.
The way they bragged me up, I thought I was one of the best.
We picked potatoes until dark, before we stopped for supper.
We were so glad to get the work, we didn't dare to mutter.

For me to stay there for the night, was their kindest wishes.
I didn't fall for their bait, I knew I'd have to do the dishes.
After supper was over, we made our way back home.
Father was very tired, but he whistled a happy tune.
I made up a song, about my day's pay.
Two cakes of homemade soap and cat coloured grey.

The basket got heavier, as I went along.
We walked every step, uphill and down.
Past the graveyard, never heard a sound.
Once in a while we'd hear a rabbit or two.
And my cat in the basket would say, Meow.

Next came Squirrel Town, a very spooky place.
It was a very dark night, and the wind was in our face.
When we got home we were all pooped out.
I took my sweater out of the basket and let out a shout.

Somewhere between Cavendish and the Mayfield Road.
Five kittens were born to add to my load.
My mother was very proud, she said indeed
What lovely kittens, just what we need.
I had a good wash with my homemade soap, and then I hit the hay.
Must be ready by five o'clock to start another day.

While riding through the African deserts, the hills of Ethiopia, Tanzania, Malawi and Zambia; then through the fertile flat lands and game farms of Botswana and Namibia; the creative side of Bernie's brain was busy composing this song. Here you see him sitting on the Gibeon Railroad Tracks in Namibia, singing his song while the film crew, who travelled with us every inch of the way, was busy capturing him on tape.

The song is sung to the tune of "Hear That Lonesome Whistle Blow" by Hank Williams.

A Warm Breeze on Our Face

We were riding on our bikes, heading south to Cape Town,
When we felt the warm breeze on our face,
We didn't trouble, had to roam; quit our jobs and left our home,
To feel the warm breeze on our face.

Just two seniors on our bikes, we know some day we'll ride a trike.
But we'll feel the warm breeze on our face.
We joined the tour just for fun, and they took all of our mon'.
But we felt the warm breeze on our face.
We're not racers, we don't fuss, If we want, we'll ride the bus.
And we'll feel the warm breeze on our face.

When we climb around the bend, and we think that is the end.
But we see the crest, another mile high in the sky.
Well we curse that very road, and we curse our heavy load.
And our pace is no faster than a toad.
But when we finally reach the top, we take a breather when we stop.
And we feel the warm breeze on our face.

When we finally reach Cape Town, we'll be up and we'll be down.
But we'll feel the warm breeze on our face.
I know that I will surely cry, but it's just a man with a tear in his eye.
And the warm breeze on his face.

LaVergne, TN USA
25 November 2009
165349LV00001B/1/P